A Time of Harvest

AMERICAN LITERATURE 1910-1960

A Time of Harvest

AMERICAN LITERATURE 1910-1960

Edited, with an introduction by

ROBERT E. SPILLER

American Century Series

HILL AND WANG · NEW YORK

Manufactured in the United States of America
by the Colonial Press Inc., Clinton, Massachusetts

Preface

DURING THE first half of the twentieth century the literature of the United States experienced a creative movement which, when it reached an equilibrium in the period between the two World Wars, produced some of the finest writing to have come from this continent in all its history.

Only once before had this happened, when the romantic movement flowered between 1835 and 1855 on the Atlantic seaboard in the work of Cooper and Irving, Poe and Emerson, Hawthorne and Melville, and Whitman. Now the impetus came from all parts of the continent, from the Atlantic to the Pacific and from the Canadian to the Mexican border, and the group of writers was larger and more diverse—Mark Twain and Henry James, Dreiser and Frost, Lewis and O'Neill, Eliot, Faulkner, Hemingway, and many more.

In each case, the literary movement in America was a part of a creative awakening in Europe, but it was clearly distinguishable from its counterparts in England, France, Italy, Germany, Russia, and Scandinavia; for the civilization of the United States differed sharply from those of Europe in that, until very recent years, it was constantly in a state of movement and flux. American culture—the whole pattern of a way of life—is a transplanted culture: it is the result of the impact of a sophisticated culture on a constantly receding wilderness. This is not true of the cultures of Europe, where the same peoples have lived in virtually the same places for more than a thousand years and have had a chance to develop their national and cultural characters from primitive beginnings up through the various stages of sophistication to the complex civilizations we know today.

The Atlantic seaboard was settled mainly by upper-middle-class educated farmers from the English midlands, who brought their literary interests with them. For two centuries, American writing, although it made valiant efforts to tell about the new experiences on the new continent—from letters home to prose epics—was modeled on the writing of English novelists, dramatists, poets, and critics. With the disrupting effects of the Civil War, the expanding frontier, the vast waves of new immigration from Continental Europe and the shift of the American economy from an agrarian to an urban and industrial base, the old culture was undermined and a new one—this time reflective of Europe in general rather than primarily of England—began to evolve.

By the end of the nineteenth century, the naturalistic movement, already highly developed in the literatures of France, Scandinavia, and Russia, began to find sympathetic reflection in a new group of American writers, many of them from the Middle and Far West and South. San Francisco, Chicago, St. Louis, and New Orleans vied with the seacoast towns from Boston to Charleston as cultural centers. Mark Twain was the first important American writer to be born west of the Mississippi, but he was not the last; Henry James was the first to take up permanent residence in Europe without sacrificing his basically American character and quality. With the naturalistic movement, American literature became both continental and cosmopolitan.

This is not the place to attempt a definition of "naturalism" except to suggest that it is the result of modern man's effort to revise his ideas of nature and of himself in accordance with what the new science seemed to have taught him. A writer must have a point of view from which to interpret his ideas and experiences and to relate them to the eternal verities; and the old assumptions no longer seemed to work. In the United States,

this intellectual and emotional revolution was further aggra-
vated by the unsettled and rapidly changing character of American society. By 1910, however, new literary modes and forms
had been developed. The next half century saw the rise, the
flowering, and the decline of naturalism in American literature,
accompanied by a vigorous critical movement which gave it
control and direction.

This is the story which this book attempts to tell—or at least
to discuss. Although the work of several hands, it was written
from a single and very full outline, and the writers of the
various chapters made their contributions with full freedom of
judgment but within a firm historical and ideological frame.
It would be too much to say that they all agree with all that
has been said in the opening paragraphs of this preface, but the
fact that they did not find the outline too restrictive to their
thought and expression may be taken as evidence of a high
degree of consensus among American literary historians today.
This was not the case in the 1940's when a similar historical
interpretation was set up, somewhat provisionally, as the structural frame of the *Literary History of the United States;* but
by now the existence and the general character of a second
literary renaissance in the United States between 1910 and 1940
is pretty much taken for granted both at home and abroad. The
exact nature, timing, scope and importance of this movement
may still be subjects for critical discussion and difference, but
the historical reality of a major literary movement in America
in this period can hardly be questioned.

The plan of this book follows an evolutionary curve in dealing with this movement. The early chapters treat of the period
from about 1910 to 1925 when the new fiction, poetry and
drama were taking shape and the critical movement was starting. Literary genres are, for the most part, discussed in separate
chapters and selected major authors are treated at length, even
at some sacrifice of total coverage. Some important writers are
therefore seemingly neglected or mentioned merely in passing
while a few appear more than once; but the book was not intended as a definitive literary history. It is rather a series of

connected and developing historical essays arranged in a more or less logical and chronological order.

The writing of the renaissance itself—from about 1925 to 1940—is then given similar treatment; and, in the last four chapters, an attempt is made at least to open up the question of what has happened since World War II and what it may mean. Obviously the impetus of the original naturalistic movement had run its course by 1945, even though many of its major authors were still living and writing, and the definitive work of the new criticism had been done. All four of the writers of these chapters have reported, without conference or previous agreement, that they sense a general breaking down of walls in both subject and form and the emergence of a new kind of individualism, related more to introspection and perhaps to European forms of existentialism than to the traditional American variety which Emerson called self-reliance. Ideas and emotions seem now to be more unsettled than they were, literary forms and fashions are looser, and experimentation in life and literature seems rampant at the same time that particularly the younger writers are earnestly on the search for norms and values. It would seem that the decline of those forces which created and shaped our second literary renaissance is leading, not to literary stagnation, but to the release of new energies, the demand for new forms and controls. The period 1910-1960 was a time of abundant literary harvest; but it closed as a time of reseeding.

R.E.S.

Acknowledgments

THE EDITOR gratefully acknowledges permission to use certain of the ideas and materials in this book as follows:

The United States Information Service and Mr. Walter Nichols, Forum Editor of the Voice of America, for the general plan and outline of this series of essays, which were originally prepared as "Forum" lecture broadcasts for overseas use.

Almqvist & Wiksell, Stockholm, Sweden, for Stephen Whicher's essay, "The Art of Poetry," from *Twelve American Poets* by Stephen Whicher and Lars Åhnebrink, copyright 1959 by Almqvist & Wiksell/Gebers Förlag AB, Stockholm.

Brandt & Brandt for lines from *Western Star* by Stephen Vincent Benét, copyright 1943 by Rosemary Carr Benét, published by Holt, Rinehart and Winston, Inc.; and lines from "The Ballad of William Sycamore" from *Selected Works of Stephen Vincent Benét*, copyright 1922 by Stephen Vincent Benét, copyright renewed 1950 by Rosemary Carr Benét.

Chandler Publishing Company for Walter Blair's essay, "The Urbanization of American Humor," based on *Native American Humor* by Walter Blair, Chapter VIII, "Twentieth-Century Humorists," copyright 1960 by Chandler Publishing Company.

City Lights Books for lines from "Howl" by Allen Ginsberg, copyright 1956 and 1959 by Allen Ginsberg.

Faber and Faber Ltd for lines from "Little Gidding" from *Four Quartets* by T. S. Eliot, copyright 1943 by T. S. Eliot.

Harcourt, Brace & World, Inc., for "Spring is like a perhaps hand" by E. E. Cummings, copyright 1925 by E. E. Cummings, reprinted from *Poems 1923-1954* by E. E. Cummings.

Holt, Rinehart and Winston, Inc., for lines from "The Ax-Helve," "Two Look at Two," "Mending Wall," and "Fire and Ice" from the *Complete Poems of Robert Frost*, copyright 1923, 1930, and 1939 by Holt, Rinehart and Winston, Inc., copyright renewed 1951 by Robert Frost; and for lines from "Chicago" and "Fish Crier" by Carl Sandburg, copyright 1916 by Holt, Rinehart and Winston, Inc., copyright renewed 1944 by Carl Sandburg.

Houghton Mifflin Company for lines from "The Avenue Bearing the Initial of Christ into the New World" from *What a Kingdom It Was* by Galway Kinnell, copyright 1960 by Galway Kinnell.

Alfred A. Knopf, Inc., for "Domination of Black" from *The Collected Poems of Wallace Stevens*, copyright 1931 and 1954 by Wallace Stevens; and for "The Operation" from *Heart's Needle* by W. D. Snodgrass, copyright 1959 by W. D. Snodgrass.

The Macmillan Company for lines from "Ben Jonson Entertains a Man from Stratford" from *Collected Poems of Edwin Arlington Robinson*, copyright 1916 by The Macmillan Company, copyright renewed by Ruth Nivison.

New Directions, Publishers, for lines from "Junkman's Obbligato" from *A Coney Island of the Mind* by Lawrence Ferlinghetti, copyright 1958 by Lawrence Ferlinghetti; for lines from "Hugh Selwyn Mauberley" from *Personae: The Collected Poems of Ezra Pound*, copyright 1926 and 1954 by Ezra Pound; and for "The Yachts" from *The Collected Earlier Poems of William Carlos Williams*, copyright 1938 and 1951 by William Carlos Williams.

The Viking Press, Inc., for "Adam" from *Letter from a Distant Land* by Philip Booth, copyright 1955 by Philip Booth.

Contributors

ROBERT E. SPILLER is author of *The American in England* and *The Cycle of American Literature* and co-editor of *Literary History of the United States*. A past President of the American Studies Association, he has lectured at numerous universities in this country and abroad and is Schelling Professor of English at the University of Pennsylvania.

WALTER BLAIR has written many books on American humor, among them *Horse Sense in American Humor*, *Mark Twain and "Huck Finn"*, and a critical anthology, *Native American Humor*. He is Professor of English at the University of Chicago.

SCULLEY BRADLEY is Professor of English and Vice-Provost of the University of Pennsylvania. He has written definitive biographies of George Henry Boker and Henry Charles Lea and is co-editor of *The American Tradition in Literature*.

TRISTRAM P. COFFIN is author of *The British Traditional Ballad in North America* and co-editor of the four-volume *Ancient Ballads Traditionally Sung in New England*. He is Secretary-Treasurer of the American Folklore Society and Associate Professor of English at the University of Pennsylvania.

DAVID DAICHES is Professor of English and Dean of the School of English and American Studies at the newly founded University of Sussex and is a Fellow of the Royal Society of Literature. He was for many years Professor of English at Cornell University and more recently University Lecturer and Fellow of Jesus College, Cambridge. Among his numerous works on the novel and literary criticism are *Critical Approaches to Literature* and *Critical History of English Literature*.

ALAN S. DOWNER is the author of *Fifty Years of American Drama*, *The Art of the Play*, and *British Drama* and is Professor of English at Princeton University. He has lectured on the modern drama at many universities at home and abroad and has twice served on the faculty of the Salzburg Seminar in American Studies in Austria.

MAXWELL GEISMAR is working on the fourth volume of *The Novel in America*, a study of major writers of fiction. A professional writer and critic, he has taught at Harvard University and Sarah Lawrence College.

C. HUGH HOLMAN, a native of South Carolina, is Professor and Chairman of the Department of English at the University of North Carolina. He is author of books and articles on Southern fiction and the history of American literary criticism.

R. W. B. LEWIS, author of *The American Adam* and *The Picaresque Saint*, is Professor of English and American Studies at Yale University. He has also served as Dean of the Salzburg Seminar in American Studies, Fulbright lecturer at Munich, and Resident Fellow in Creative Writing and Criticism at Princeton and Rutgers Universities.

ARTHUR MIZENER is author of the biography of F. Scott Fitzgerald, *The Far Side of Paradise*, and a frequent contributor to the literary quarterlies. He is Professor of English at Cornell University.

NORMAN HOLMES PEARSON is Chairman of the Department of American Studies at Yale University, co-editor of *The Oxford Anthology of American Literature* and, with W. H. Auden, the five-volume *Poets of the English Language*. He received decorations from the American, French, and Norwegian governments for distinguished service in World War II.

HENRY POPKIN taught at Rutgers and Brandeis Universities and at the Universities of Clermont-Ferrand and Lyon in France before becoming Associate Professor of English at New York University. He has written on modern drama and the mass media for *The New York Times Magazine, Commentary,* and other periodicals.

WILLARD THORP is Holmes Professor of Belles Lettres and Chairman of the Department of English at Princeton University. In addition to works on Elizabethan drama and English poetry, he has co-edited *The American Literary Record* and *Literary History of the United States* and edited *A Southern Reader*.

GERALD WEALES also contributes criticism of contemporary drama to the *Reporter, Commonweal, Kenyon Review,* and other periodicals. He taught at Wayne State and Brown Universities before joining the English faculty at the University of Pennsylvania. He is the author of *Religion in Modern Drama* and the novel, *Tale for the Bluebird*.

STEPHEN E. WHICHER was the author of *Freedom and Fate*, a critical study of Ralph Waldo Emerson, and co-editor of Emerson's *Early Lectures*. Professor of English at Cornell University, he edited, with Lars Åhnebrink of the University of Uppsala, Sweden, the anthology, *Twelve American Poets*, upon which his essay in this volume is based. He died in late 1961.

Contents

A Time of Harvest
AMERICAN LITERATURE 1910-1960

ROBERT E. SPILLER

1: The Critical Rediscovery of America

"IT WAS only the other day," said Van Wyck Brooks in 1921, "that America first came in for its effective share of self-criticism. The critical movement happened, as it were, overnight." Far from being a symptom of disillusionment, the new self-critical attitude, Mr. Brooks thought, was an evidence of a new faith—the faith of modern Americans in their power to shape their own destiny—"to ride things as things have ridden them." The old faith had been based on the assumption that everything in nature is congenial to the best interests of the human race and that, for this reason, it is best to allow events and ideas to take their own course. Such a philosophy was very fitting to an expanding and moving civilization, but when the continental limits have been reached, when at least certain of the vast natural resources like virgin timber have been exhausted, and when immigration has been severely restricted, a new and more nearly critical philosophy becomes inevitable.

The first step in developing such a philosophy was the assertion of the act of criticism itself. It was Brooks who first used the term "Literary Radical" to describe his contemporary, Randolph Bourne, as a leader with the courage to turn against the nineteenth-century literary tradition and to declare the revolt of twentieth-century American youth.

That tradition was one, thought these young men, of a too-

1

great dependence on Europe, and particularly on England. "Our cultural humility," wrote Bourne in 1914, "is the chief obstacle. . . . With our eyes fixed on Europe, we continue to strangle whatever native genius springs up."

At this same time Brooks was calling for the rejection of those literary standards which had made Cooper seem an American Scott, and Bryant an American Wordsworth, and had turned the limpid poetry of Longfellow into a watered-down version of German and English romantic songs and tales. We must, he felt, as Emerson and Hawthorne had felt many years before, discover our own "usable past" and vital present. Walt Whitman, of all the earlier American writers, had come nearest to showing the way, and Americans had been the last to accept Whitman's challenge.

H. L. Mencken was perhaps the most colorful and forceful of these Literary Radicals. The son of a German cigar maker in Baltimore, he learned about America by reporting for the newspapers of that city which he made his lifetime home. An experimental book on Nietzsche allowed him to work out his own ideas on iconoclasm. When he became editor of the *Smart Set* magazine, and later the *American Mercury*, he acquired a rostrum from which to bombard the deferences, the inhibitions, and the pruderies that seemed to him to be strangling American life.

Mencken did not invent the idea that puritanism was at the root of the trouble, but he hammered at it with as much vim as did anybody. It was from our earnest ancestors—so the theory ran—that we inherited both an idealism that shut out any chance of knowing the facts of life and a materialism that prevented any chance of realizing our ideals. But we were learning rapidly, Mencken thought, as writers like Theodore Dreiser could testify.

Mencken's essay on Dreiser—still the most vigorous and valid defense of that controversial literary giant—became the rallying point for the critical warfare of the era. Literary conservatives and literary radicals alike sharpened their critical tools by taking sides on the Dreiser question, and one critic—Stuart Sherman—ended by revising his first position and writing convincing essays on both sides of the argument. For Dreiser had, as early as 1900 in the suppressed novel *Sister Carrie*, declared that life in modern America could be genuinely tragic, and that goodness is not always rewarded, evil punished, in the affairs of men. Mencken made it clear that the earlier optimistic and proper "realism" of William Dean Howells did not strike at the heart of reality at all. Under the pioneering leadership of Dreiser, he urged all young American novelists to deal with the basic human drives of sex and money without glossing over the ugly and the tragic consequences of man's follies. How well the succeeding generations of American novelists learned this lesson is demonstrated in Hemingway and Faulkner, Mailer and Kerouac.

This was a literary criticism to release pent-up energies rather than to control and direct them. It was vitally needed at the time it appeared—that is, just before and during World War I —but it was basically romantic, impressionistic, and provocative rather than judicial and evaluative. The one critical principle that it contributed was the belief that literature, to be authentic, must be a direct expression of the society that produces it. This is realism in a more fundamental sense than the earlier American writers, even Mark Twain, had known. It was a call to modern writers to start again from the roots of experience and to make of literature the profound criticism of life that great art must always be. Literary and social criticism—at least in this phase of the American reawakening—could not be divorced.

The two most influential critics that this point of view produced were the historian Vernon L. Parrington and the free-lance journalist Edmund Wilson.

Parrington's *Main Currents in American Thought*, when it appeared in 1927, shocked readers and scholars alike and reshaped the whole accepted concept of American literary history. Up to then, it had been assumed that American literature, because it was largely written in the English language, was a mere part of English literature. Parrington pointed first to those writers of the colonial and Revolutionary periods in our history who had created, from their experience with the frontier and their arguments about the basic principles of human society, a distinctive American social philosophy. This, he believed, was the agrarian democratic system of Thomas Jefferson. He then proceeded to line up American writers according to their relationship, pro and con, with this view.

The result was a reshuffling, with writers like Cooper, Thoreau, Whitman, and Mark Twain—who dealt directly with American experience—moving to the top, and writers like Poe and James, Lowell and Longfellow—who dealt rather with abstractions and idealizations—falling from grace. This was one version of the "usable past" that Brooks and others had called for, an essential reorientation of American thinking about America's own cultural inheritance.

It was not until two decades later that a group of literary historians and critics, working from a modified Parringtonian base of the relationship of literature to society, could produce, in the *Literary History of the United States*, a total reappraisal in philosophical and aesthetic as well as political and social terms. The culture itself had to be redefined before its literary expression, through the long years of its growth, could be described and judged.

The forces which brought American historical critics to terms with these broader truths were largely the ideological battles of the thirties which preceded the outbreak of World War II. Parrington was right in his belief that American literature must first be understood as the expression of American civilization, but he was wrong in his own understanding of that civilization as it had developed in the twentieth century. An urbanized, industrialized world power could not continue to live by the ideals of an agrarian and colonial inheritance. The Literary Radicals were soon forced to face the further issue: if literature must express its society, what kind of society could and should the United States make for itself now? The powerful forces of Fascism and Communism grimly challenged the democratic inheritance, and many American poets, novelists, and dramatists lost their literary bearings in an attempt to take sides on what were basically political issues.

Among American literary critics, Edmund Wilson perhaps

best steered his way through the ideological turmoil of the thirties. Drawn so far toward the extremes of psychological and social theory as to write excellent treatments of both Freudianism and Communism, Wilson never lost sight of his own role as a literary critic and as a critic of modern American literature. There are few American literary critics of those days who would now dare to do what Wilson has done: collect his essays, exactly as they appeared, into volumes by decades and offer them as a historical chronicle of ideas. The secret of his success is that he has always had the gift of liking the right books for the right reasons, and he has therefore been able to make an amazing record of critical bull's eye hits.

An old law of physics holds that every action produces a reaction, equal in force and opposite in direction. Literary history is no exception to this rule, and a vigorously dynamic movement such as that of the Literary Radicals must soon produce a more exacting critical response leading to neoclassical standards, forms, and controls.

Among the people with whom Mencken most vigorously crossed swords were Irving Babbitt and J. E. Spingarn, both of them professors of modern literature—the one at Harvard, the other at Columbia—and both literary theorists rather than literary critics. Babbitt and Spingarn, although as violently in revolt against the nineteenth century as any of the Literary Radicals, differed from Brooks, Bourne, and Mencken in their insistence on moral or aesthetic rather than political or social criteria for literary judgment. They were philosophers rather than historians of literature, and their criticism was speculative and judicial.

It was George Santayana who identified the Neohumanist movement which Babbitt sponsored with what he christened the Genteel Tradition, the last stand of nineteenth-century ideals. He was right in feeling that Babbitt, Paul Elmer More, and their followers agreed with the earlier idealists in fighting a world of mindless natural laws. In opposing Mencken, Dreiser, and most of the Literary Radicals, the two groups would have agreed, but the Neohumanists differed from their predecessors in that they were militant and aggressive, whereas the "genteel" critics merely shone in the afterglow of Emersonian brilliance.

Babbitt's arch foes were what he called the "old romanticism" and the "new science." "It may be," he ventured, "that criticism is something more than Mr. Mencken would have us believe. . . . The serious critic is more concerned with achieving a correct scale of values and so seeing things proportionately than with self-expression." Mencken's kind of criticism he dismissed as "superior intellectual vaudeville."

The romantics, he believed, had turned the individual loose in a meaningless world to shift for himself without moral law or reason for guide, and the new scientists had further compounded the confusion by demonstrating that natural law is both meaningless and all-powerful. For more than a century, Babbitt protested, English and American literature had drifted, and now at least the Americans were in a morass of sensory impressions and responses.

What was the answer? Not to turn back from science to God, for that would be merely substituting one arbitrary and nonhuman rule for another. The medieval Humanists had revolted against the dictates of an arbitrary deity and had used scientific inquiry to establish the authority of the human will. Now science had become equally dictatorial and the human will was again in jeopardy. The job to be done was to swing the pendulum back to a position of poise. The Humanists must once more in a dualistic world find a way in which man could control the affairs of man without deference to super- or sub-human authority.

The Neohumanist movement in its extreme and dogmatic form came to a head about 1930 and more or less burned itself out; but its stimulus to a rethinking of the fundamental problems of literature and morality had a profound and lasting influence. The contribution of Irving Babbitt and his fellows to American critical thinking lay not so much in their attacks on Mencken and the Literary Radicals as in their knowledge of the best classical and European critical thought and literature. Even against their will, they joined forces with the Literary Radicals in freeing American literature from its hampering and exclusive link with the "English literature" tradition.

It was said that Babbitt's students, in his classes at Harvard, used to amuse themselves by counting his allusions to world literature and, on one occasion, tallied seventy within an hour. The French, German, and classical sources of literary theory and criticism could once again flow, as they had in the days of Emerson, into the American creative consciousness without being filtered first through the British critics and reviews. The reactionary and fundamentalist wing of the American critical movement had made its own contribution to the reawakening of the national literary consciousness. The ancients and the moderns had joined forces in a new Battle of the Books.

One more—a third—school of literary criticism emerged from the battles of these years, a way of thinking which was much less influential at the time than that of the Literary Radicals and the Neohumanists but which soon came to be perhaps the most important of all for its contribution to what later came to be called the "New Criticism." This was the aesthetic impressionism of J. E. Spingarn, a student of the Renaissance and of the Italian critic Croce. Spingarn drew his ideas from the same sources as did the Neohumanists, that is, the mainstream of the classical and European literary tradition, but he reached somewhat different conclusions. He stressed, as the primary function of literature, not the expression of its own society and times, like the Literary Radicals, nor the basic moral values of all times, like the Neohumanists, but the act of imaginative creation itself. Echoing Goethe, Carlyle, and Sainte-Beuve, he directed attention to the work of art in itself and in its relationships to its author and its reader, asking what the poet tried to do, how he fulfilled his intentions, and how he was received. But he hastened to add: "The poet's intentions must be judged at the moment of the creative act, as mirrored in the work of art itself, and not by the vague ambitions which he imagines to be his real intentions before or after the creative act is achieved."

This is, of course, an essentially romantic approach to literary criticism and would link Spingarn with Brooks and Mencken rather than with Babbitt and More, but its immediate result was to call attention to the work of art rather than to any aspect of its context and so prepare the way for the more disciplined analytical critics who were to come later.

Thus, all the major questions with which literary criticism can legitimately be concerned had been asked by 1920 and had been vigorously fought over. But the most important result of all this critical activity was not that it developed a distinctive school of literary criticism—which it did—but that it provided the foundation structures for a literary renaissance. The American writer of the twenties and thirties no longer felt the "cultural humility" which Brooks and Bourne had deplored in 1915. He could lash out at his own society, as Theodore Dreiser, Sinclair Lewis, and John Dos Passos proceeded to do, with as much confidence and vigor as a Swift or a Voltaire; he could search for the tragic inevitabilities of all life, as did Faulkner, O'Neill, and Wolfe, in his own experience without danger of provincialism; and he could respond to his own lyric stirrings, like a Frost or an Eliot, without reaching beyond the language, the learning, the firsthand experience, and the idiom of his times for a borrowed form of expression. American literature, by pushing its roots deeper and more firmly into the past, was at last discovering its own things to say and its own ways of saying them. Truly, it had "come of age."

TRISTRAM P. COFFIN

2: The Heritage of Folklore

ONE OF THE first evidences of this new self-aware-
ness was an upsurge of interest in the tales and songs of the
American folk. The peoples of the world possess two types of
literature: written and oral. Written literature consists of the
material that appears in books and is read by persons of some
education. Oral literature is made up of the material that men
and women pass on to each other by word of mouth generation after generation. Among a primitive group like the American Indians or the African Bushmen, all the literature is oral.
In a society such as that of twentieth-century America, most
of the literature is written down, although there is a large body
of matter (songs, tales, legends, games, rhymes, jokes, proverbs,
riddles, and superstitions) that people learn from their parents,
grandparents, and friends, that they don't write down, and that
they never will write down. This matter is the folklore of a
modern, civilized nation—and while it is obvious that the less
schooling a person has the more likely he is to preserve what he
knows of oral literature, even the most highly educated citizen
will recall some folklore.

All nations have rich folk heritages, and America offers no
exception. Nevertheless, America is a country with a high level
of mass education and a vast network of mass communication.
As more and more Americans read, listen to the radio, and

9

watch television, fewer and fewer of them bother to learn folklore from memory. Therefore, during the last fifty years the United States has shown a steadily increasing interest in what is a vanishing cultural heritage. American collectors have worked feverishly to uncover and preserve as much of the national folklore as possible before it is all forgotten. The job has been done, on the whole, well. Today, most of the rich and varied folklore of the United States is recorded in books or on tapes and records, and is available in library archives. Publishers edit and mass-distribute it; schools and colleges teach and analyze it; writers develop and embellish it.

However, folklore is like leaves from a tree or shells from the shore. Take it away from its natural surroundings and it fades and loses its full beauty. Folklore flourishes only when it is an oral tradition, where people interchange it and listen to it without recording it in a set, never-to-change-again form. As they relate it or sing it from memory and as others learn it, folklore lives, varying and developing as the people forget parts of it, add parts to it, and adapt parts of it to suit their fancies. This process, which is called oral variation, is the life-blood of folklore. When the process is halted by printing or recording, the folklore involved ceases to be alive, just as the leaf pressed in the book or the shell sitting on the table is no longer its "real self." Thus, no matter how popular folklore becomes in America, one has to face the fact that American folklore is dying out in this land where more and more citizens use writing and mass communications as a way of expressing their feelings about life.

The fact that folklore is losing its vitality in the United States does not mean that it is unimportant, however, for in it we can still see the dreams and fears and desires of the people who built this country out of a wilderness or who emigrated to this country to get a fresh start. As these people were, at first, mostly from the British Isles, it is to be expected that the mainstream of American folklore, like Americans themselves, is going to be largely British in background. To be sure, peoples of many other lands have helped build America, but it is also true that in general as they have come to this country they have mixed with the British and allowed their own national heritage to slip away from them over the years. Negro lore, for instance, was originally a mixture of Moorish and African elements, but today is dominated by all sorts of British matter. Nevertheless, one must not forget that along our borders, French to the north and Spanish to the southwest, and in our cities, where many Asiatics, Europeans, and Islanders are gathered, immigrant lores flourish untouched by Anglo-American traditions and patterns.

Culturally, America is extremely diverse. It is also a nation that came into being rapidly and recently. In a nation such as this, it is dangerous to insist that a national folklore, even of British background, exists in any real sense. Certainly a folklorist would be bold to attempt to treat American folklore as a whole. One does best to follow lines of division—perhaps essentially ethnic ones like those drawn by the American Folklore Society at the time of its founding in 1888. The Society broke American folklore into these parts: (1) relics of British lore; (2) Negro lore; (3) American Indian lore; (4) lore of recent, unacculturated ethnic groups (the French, the Spanish, the Swedes, and so forth). Such a division marks well the main areas of labor that American folklorists have observed in the twentieth century.

However, this is but an initial breakdown. All folk groups in America are affected by their social and economic positions, their levels of education, and their relationships to mass communications. What the various groups accept and reject, what their local attachments are, how reliant they are on their particular traditional practices and heritages—such factors cause a complex cultural interplay within the United States that is almost too intricate to conceive.

The result is that one has to consider regional and occupational divisions along with the ethnic ones. Where a group of distinct racial and linguistic stock exists in some sort of cultural isolation, it will develop regional characteristics that may be more marked than the ethnic ones. This is the case, for example, of the British mountain whites, the Afro-American Negroes of the coastal islands of Georgia and South Carolina, the Pennsylvania Dutch, the Louisiana French, and the New England Yankees. The same is true when the work of the group has led toward isolation extending over long periods. Sailing, lumbering, river-boating, canaling, grazing, railroading, mining, even pioneering are cases in point. In addition, regionalism and occupation frequently combine with ethnic individualities to foster particularly distinct lores such as the southern slave songs, Mormon tradition, northern metropolitan Negro toasts, the spirituals of the southern upland whites, and the songs of the Shakers.

Thus one can see that the discussion of even a single ballad or a single superstition in America is a complicated discussion, which may lead up all sorts of ethnic, regional, and occupational paths. On the one hand, the same song or story may turn up in many places among many different groups, displaying some slight local touches. For example, the British music hall ballad, "The Bad Girl's Lament," which tells of the degeneration and death of a prostitute, can be traced throughout the United States, in the hills as a moral lyric, in the Southwest as a dirge about a cowboy who has gone wrong, and among the Negroes as a city blues or "sorrow song." A rhyme like "Eeny meeny miny mo/ Catch a nigger by the toe/ If he hollers let him go/ Eeny meeny miny mo" reflects Celtic shepherd chants, French-Canadian children's games, the Negro-white relationships during the days before the Civil War. On the other hand, it is indisputably true that each region, each occupation, and each racial group has preserved a genuine body of lore that is inseparable from local culture. Tales about place names, about local feuds and loyalties, and about local features have arisen wherever people have noticed that they are different from each other. Frequently, such place lore becomes interlaced with history, as in the South, where colonial, plantation, Civil War, and Reconstruction days all have their respective symbols, heroes, and legends.

To describe even briefly the many literary forms that American folklore takes would be a tedious process. The list of folk-song types alone in the United States would include three kinds of Anglo-American narrative songs or ballads; the Spanish narrative *corrido;* an infinite variety of dance and game lyrics; Negro calls, blues, spirituals, and hollers; work songs of many sorts; hymns and white spirituals; primitive Indian chants and prayers; and the various European and British love lyrics. A list of folk-tale types would include European *Märchen;* trickster tales of the Negro and the Indian; numbskull tales of the French and Spanish; local legends concerning ghosts, place names, and geographical features of all sorts; tall tales; primitive Indian myths; and European endless, accumulative, and formula stories. In addition, there are superstitions, sayings, proverbs, and jokes that go with every occupation, racial group, and region in the nation, besides an infinite variety of games, dances, rhymes, and such things. Folk forms the world over differ very little, and what one finds in the United States is just about what he would expect to find in any Western nation, with the exception of Negro folk music and the frontier tall tale. The distinguishing features of American folklore are not so much in form as in the close interplay of racial and regional groups, in the steady influence of print and commercialism, and in the ever-changing nature of American society.

America is, of course, the melting pot of the world. In America, people of all races, creeds, and languages have mixed their blood, their cultures, and their hopes. Folklore in a real sense symbolizes this union, and there is an obvious democratic appeal in the fact that American oral literature is too complex for simple description, that American songs or tales move from group to group transcending ethnic, linguistic, and intellectual barriers.

Actually, the growth of interest in folklore in America stands in direct proportion to the growth of American influence across the world. During the years surrounding the two World Wars, the United States has been concerned with its own heritage as it has gone about the job of explaining itself to other peoples. Scholars, writers, and entertainers have fed the public desire to know their neighbors and to know themselves. The complex of folklore has offered an appropriate and endless source of supply.

Perhaps the best way to understand the popularity of folk-lore in America from 1910 to 1955 is to look at the people who are the folklorists themselves. As one might expect, they are a mixed breed. Anthropologists, housewives, historians, litera-ture teachers by profession, they have approached their disci-pline as amateurs, collectors, commercialists, and scholars, or as some combination of the four. They are of widely varying backgrounds and tastes, and as a group share little *esprit de corps*.

The outlook for the amateur, for instance, is usually de-pendent on his fondness for local history or the picturesque. His love of folklore has romanticism in it, and may reflect nostalgia for "the good old days" or simply love of his home town or ancestor's race. Folklore is his hobby, and he, all too rightly, insists that it remain as such. The amateur is closely related to the collector, who is actually the amateur who has taken to the field. The collector enjoys contact with people; he hunts folklore for the very "field and stream" reasons that many persons hunt game. Only rarely is he acutely concerned with the meaning of what he has located. During the early years of the twentieth century, when it was first realized that American folklore was vanishing, he had his great era.

But there are also the commercialists and the scholars—one dominated by money, the other by a desire to discover the truth about American life and culture. Both are primarily con-cerned with the uses that can be made of the material the collector has brought home. Both shudder at the thought of proceeding too far beyond the sewage system and the electric light lines. The commercialist gets along well with the amateur, on whose nostalgias he feeds, but he frequently steps on the toes of the scholar by refusing to keep his material genuine. He wants to tinker with and embellish folklore in order to give it the greatest commercial appeal. His standards are com-pletely foreign to those of the scholar. To both the amateur and the commercialist, the scholar lacks a soul, lacks appreciation with his endless probings and classifications. Dominated by the vicious circle of the university promotion system, the scholar looks down on and gets along poorly with the other three groups, although he cannot deny his debt to the collector.

In the years from 1910 to 1955 all of these types have been able to flourish and develop their distinctions. The amateurs, the commercialists, and the collectors have brought out book after book and record after record of the folklore of almost every conceivable ethnic, regional, and occupational group in America. The scholars have probed the complicated histories of British ballads like "The Maid Freed from the Gallows," American Negro songs like "John Henry," American Indian myths like "The Star Husband," French customs like *La Guillannée*, and so forth. The groups have warred over the legitimacy of rearranging folk songs, over the ritual connections of myths and tales, over the folk groups that can claim to have originated this song and that game. The result has been a mass of books of varying quality that crowd our libraries, the successful launchings of four major and a host of minor folklore journals, a surfeit of records of folk songs and folk dances, a rapid development of courses in all aspects of American and world folklore throughout American schools and colleges.

To be sure, the knowledge that most Americans have of folklore has come through contact with the commercialists, who have reached the largest audience. The work done by the collectors and the scholars, the men who deeply care about folk literature, has had the limited appeal that any other work of a truly scientific sort always has. As a result, while the American public has been exposed to huge amounts of its folk heritage in recent years, most Americans have a rather hazy idea of what folklore really is. They have been exposed to folklore not as it was originally taken from the mouths of folk informants, but rather after it has been modified that it may sell. Folklore is almost always objective, amoral, and cruel when found in its natural state; folk songs are often in archaic keys and difficult to listen to; much of the narrative matter is obscene. However, when it is presented on American phonograph records and over American bookstore counters, it is certain to be sentimental, moral, and even cute, the music transposed into familiar modes and dressed up with commercial clichés, the obscenities glossed over. Thus, most Americans have little idea of the power, energy, and originality that lies in their folklore. Rather they see it as quaint, entertaining, and of passing value.

If we look at what has happened commercially to American folk song in the last fifty years, we can get a pretty clear idea of what all forms of American folklore have been subjected to since World War I. The details may differ for folk tales or for superstitions, but the pattern will not vary much from form to form.

In the twentieth century, there have been three big commercial movements that have caused a great interest in folk song singing in the United States. The first of these is the hillbilly movement. When record companies learned after World War I that the public would buy recordings of songs by country folk, they went to rural areas and recorded singers. These singers were mostly British upland whites from the Ozark and Southern Appalachian regions. The songs they sang were genuine Anglo-American folk songs. However, it was soon found that it was easier to bring the country folk to the city or to have city singers imitate the country style. From these imitations the tradition of hillbilly singing grew up. Now most of the songs sung by hillbilly singers are written by men in the music business. Their mood is sentimental, moral, and monotonous, where the folk song is stark, indifferent, and varied. Thousands upon thousands of them are played and sung over American mass media outlets. The hill country is flooded with them and today even the hill singers prefer them to the more traditional songs. Although hillbilly singing is often equated in the mind of the American public with folk singing, the relationship is now extremely distant except in a few isolated cases.

The second great movement is the labor movement. Late in the nineteenth century and early in the twentieth, union organizers discovered that folk songs had great appeal to the workers in the factories and mines as they struggled to better their lot. Soon the singing of folk songs about hardship, the rewriting of folk songs so they dealt with hardship, and the composing of songs in the folk manner was being encouraged as a means of protesting against big business and the advantages big businessmen were taking of the employees. During the late thirties this vogue of singing appropriate and doctored folk songs spread from the unions to a wider audience interested in a broader protest of a political and social nature. Influenced by current popular musical trends, such songs reached a broader and broader audience and eventually began to vie with the products of dance music and hillbilly writers for the attention of record buyers and radio-TV listeners. By the 1950's almost any group dressing in a rural fashion and calling itself a folk group could perform this music and be assured of steady engagements and a good crop of listeners.

Finally, jazz has brought to America's radio stations and television outlets a great many Negro folk songs. Jazz, which began in New Orleans as a mixture of Negro field calls and spirituals, country and urban "sorrow songs" or blues, European band music, and various piano styles, has swept over the nation and the world. Wherever it is played, the blues are sung—and the blues are a genuine form of American folk song. Rising from the playing and singing of the Negroes, especially the street singers in the southern towns and cities, the blues originally expressed the sadness and hardship of lonely blacks in a white man's world. Later the whites took over the form to express their own trouble and pain. As the Negroes and the hillbillies came north and went into the entertainment business, they brought the blues with them. The blues have been popular on the radio and in night clubs; they have been copied and rewritten by whites and blacks alike; and they have lived in their folk form in the Negro districts of the huge cities and southern farm lands.

However, if we are to survey a form, such as the folk song, to observe the steady commercialization of American folklore from 1910 to 1955, we ought also to look at a form, such as the tall tale, to observe the basic American characteristics that reveal themselves in the face of the regional, occupational, and ethnic distinctions. The tall tale developed in rural America and on the frontier during the early nineteenth century. A loose, rambling story of personal experience, this typically American form of anecdote-telling is presented casually, in an offhand manner, with utmost solemnity in the face of the most preposterous incidents. Much of the detail is irrelevant; the climax is usually bathetic; and the purpose is really to "take in" the listener. Hoaxes, marvels, and scrapes are the tall-tale teller's stock in trade.

The tall tale is, of course, uniquely American, a true product of the many races and groups that flooded onto our western frontier. Its heroes are divided between the prosaic Yankee—whose virtues are industry, perseverance, thrift, know-how, and cunningness—and the western brawler—whose virtues are courage, brawn, brute force, and animal cleverness. These heroes are a picaresque type of footloose adventurer, the result and symbol of a society cut loose from its roots. In the thin line that separates law-enforcement from law-breaking on the frontier, both the good bad man and the bad good man are glorified. Davy Crockett tricks the barkeep by trading the same coonskin again and again for drinks, he grins the bark off a tree, rassles bears, and ends up in Congress. Mike Fink squabbles, drinks, and robs his way along the Mississippi, but helps an honest man get a start in life. Wild Bill Hickok shoots his initials in telegraph poles as he rides by, and is himself shot in the back.

These are the stories from American folklore that the American public knows best and likes best. The frontier ideal of the resourceful, outdoor individualist is far preferred to the character types that emerge from the European *Märchen*, from the Negro animal story, and from the other narrative forms the folk have to offer. America has always been proud of its star performers, its master workmen, and its lusty, blustering champions, and it pays continual tribute to the heroes that have arisen from our tall tales. States claim to be the home of Pecos Bill, the marvelous cowboy, or of Paul Bunyan, the wonder-working lumberman. Negroes name their children after John Henry of steel-driving fame. Festivals and carnivals honor the apple-planter Johnny Appleseed, or the railroad daredevil Casey Jones.

Although folk songs and tall tales have had the greatest commercial distribution in the United States and thus have become the best-known types of folk literature, this does not mean that other forms have not had their distribution too. Most Americans are familiar with Old World *Märchen* taken from the mountain whites, the French, and the Spanish; with the trickster stories of the African Negro, if not with the trickster stories of the American Indian; with dance games derived from the frontier square dances and play-parties; with local superstitions and customs, such as dowsing or water-witching, prophesying weather, curing warts, and controlling luck; with a few riddles, rhymes, and jokes; and with the legends characteristic of their native groups. A few have seen *Los Pastores*, the medieval Spanish dramas still acted in the Southwest; the French New Year's celebration, *La Guillannée*; or some other traditional ceremony. Folk festivals and folk carnivals of one sort or another have grown quite popular in the United States, and each year sees ethnic, regional, and occupational groups displaying their customs and costumes, telling their tales, dancing and singing their songs in an effort to promote better understanding and mutual self-respect in this polyglot nation. For example, the National Folk Festival held every spring in the South brings together performers, scholars, and amateurs of folklore from all over the country and is given wide publicity in newspapers and magazines, while each month some group—the lumbermen, the Finns, the mountain whites, an American Indian tribe—holds some sort of revival or carnival.

One may conclude from this discussion of folklore in the United States from 1910 to 1955 that three theses have emerged: (1) that American folklore is an exceptionally complex and intricate interplay of regional, occupational, and ethnic forces; (2) that the great vogue of American folklore is related to our desire to explain ourselves to the world; and (3) that folklore has been ever-increasingly commercialized as its popularity has grown. And one realizes that American folklore has developed in an age of print and rapid national change when the urges of nostalgia and local pride have been strong. As a result, Americans have been extraordinarily anxious to retain for posterity as much of their heritage as possible. They have treasured more carefully than other lands local traditions, memories, and bric-a-brac. While this preservation has often been helter-skelter, the storehouse of American lore built up is amazingly full.

What is in this storehouse does symbolize the nation. America is a new, young, big land, mirroring rapid changes from agricultural to urban life. The people are a mixture. So is the culture. In America, men have become heroes in their own lifetimes and living storytellers encompass within their memories the entire history of a community or a profession such as canaling or river-boating. Such a nation is all things to all people and immensely difficult to label. Its folklore is endlessly fascinating, if impossible to define.

3: The Renaissance in Poetry

IT WAS in the more formal poetry, fiction, and drama
of the new century that the signs of a renaissance were first
fully apparent. While the genteel poets of the *fin de siècle* such
as Stedman and Gilder mimicked the past, or, like Richard
Hovey, optimistically sang that "It's always fair weather," or,
like Field and Riley, turned to *vers de société* and other patri-
cian, comic, or familiar light verse, two poets of the modern
temper had struggled unheard. One was William Vaughn
Moody, who died in 1910 at the age of forty; the other was
his coeval, Edwin Arlington Robinson, who lived through the
later flood tide of the revival, one of its greatest and most
disturbing voices, and one of its clearly great poets.

From these and from independent sources a group of
younger poets drew their inspiration; before 1916 serious
American readers were excitedly aware of a chorus of "new
voices," characterized by vitality and independence, differing
greatly from each other while speaking the same language of
artistic urgency beamed at a public whom they commanded to
listen. Pound's first *Personae* (1909) coincided with the initial
shock of Gertrude Stein; in 1910, after a decade of silence,
Robinson published *The Town Down the River*; by 1916
Amy Lowell had published two controversial volumes; Vachel
Lindsay had revitalized balladry with *General William Booth*

21

and *The Congo*; Frost had won a phenomenal acceptance in England and the Untied States with *A Boy's Will, North of Boston*, and *Mountain Interval*; Edgar Lee Masters had published the revolutionary *Spoon River Anthology*, and Sandburg his radical *Chicago Poems*. Voices from the past, a posthumous volume of Emily Dickinson and the collected works of Whitman, qualified these radical poets as "modernists." Soon there were American magazines specializing in poetry and enlivened by the early poems of Eliot, Frost, Sandburg, Pound, Edna Millay, "H.D.," William Carlos Williams, Marianne Moore, Jeffers, Wallace Stevens, and MacLeish. This flowering of poetry in the decade before World War I has, not without reason, been called the Little Renaissance.

In the present chapter the period as a whole will be represented by three poets whose best work approaches greatness. These poets are Robinson, Frost, and Sandburg; and in addition a somewhat younger poet, Stephen Vincent Benét, should be included, since his short-lived creativeness produced a unique contribution. Each of these poets was deeply concerned to express the immediate condition and daily lives of mankind in a new poetry appropriate for this century's violence and upheaval, its hunger for understanding and wisdom. Robert Frost remembered of his beginnings that he "had a lover's quarrel with the world"; Sandburg and Robinson might have described their motivations more violently.

With this generation of poets the United States found a continental voice. The twentieth-century poets had roots in California, Arizona, and the Mississippi Valley as well as in Maine, Massachusetts, and the old South. Robinson Jeffers, laureate of the California hills, grew up in western Pennsylvania, and Frost, destined to interpret New England, spent his boyhood in California. For a time it seemed that the Middle West would become the crucible of the new poetry. Carl Sandburg, Vachel Lindsay, and Edgar Lee Masters found each other in Chicago, new Mecca for writers of the Upper Midlands. Sara Teasdale and T. S. Eliot grew up in St. Louis on the upper Mississippi. It was in Chicago that the first American magazine exclusively for poets, *Poetry: A Magazine of Verse*, appeared in 1912, just when the first poets of the Little Renaissance were seeking to be heard. Standard American magazines—*Harper's*, *Scribner's*, or the *Atlantic Monthly*, for example—had become guardians of the established tradition, but the new magazine was hospitable to all good poetry whether radical or traditional.

There was a richness and variety in the new lyric repertoire of the United States. Vachel Lindsay's "big bass drum" and his Congolese "boomlay, boom" was in curious counterpoint with the "sculptured" precision of Pound, Eliot, or Hilda Doolittle ("H.D."); with the restrained and witty intellectualism of Robinson; with the humanely tempered "fire and ice" of Robert Frost; with the ennobled vernacular of Sandburg; with Amy Lowell's "free verse," "sprung rhythm," and "polyphonic prose"; with love poems by Miss Teasdale or Miss Millay, traditional in form but in Freudian sensibility recalling Sappho's American avatar, Emily Dickinson, the precocious spinster of Amherst, Massachusetts, who died securely unpublished in 1886. Sandburg's variations upon Whitman's "barbaric yawp" were welcomed early in the *Poetry* magazine, where he described his city, Chicago, in the language of advertising:

> Hog Butcher for the World,
> Tool Maker, Stacker of Wheat,
> Player with Railroads and the Nation's Freight Handler;
> Stormy, husky, brawling,
> City of the Big Shoulders:

Imagism was only the most boisterous and confident of many "schools" of poetry that appeared with overnight abundance like wild flowers on a spring-awakened meadow. They hurled their "manifestoes" not only at each other, but at a myriad of other "schools"—vorticist, veritist, vers-librist; Freudian, intellectualist, naturalistic; the nihilists of the *Blast* group of the classicists and traditionalists—all had their programs; many took to the lecture platform as Amy Lowell did with mammoth impressiveness. Collectively they shocked the public into an awareness, enlarged the concepts of poetry, and restored its formal richness and variety. They learned from each other. The Imagists generally practiced free verse, but Sandburg discovered

it in Whitman, and although he was not of the Imagistic group
he gave us the perfection of free-verse Imagism in "Fog":

> The fog comes
> on little cat feet.
>
> It sits looking
> over harbor and city
> on silent haunches
> and then moves on.

The inherent threat in this poem, the suggestion that nature
harbors a lurking enmity toward man, is characteristic of the
pessimistic determinism which thoughtful American writers
then expressed. In an earlier age, with all the gusto of romanticism, Whitman wrote, about 1855, "I exist as I am, that is
enough, . . . My foothold is tenon'd and mortis'd in granite,
I laugh at what you call dissolution, and I know the amplitude
of time." Such cosmic optimism was not available for Stephen
Crane, about 1890, when he wrote:

> A man said to the universe:
>   "Sir, I exist!"
> "However," replied the universe,
> "That fact has not created in me
> A sense of obligation."

This conflict between faith and doubt among the poets of the
early twentieth century was a persistent motivation. In Eliot's
The Waste Land (1922) or Robinson's *The Man Against the
Sky* (1916) it was the subject of a major work. It was a
recurrent note for Frost, Sandburg, Masters, and Jeffers; for
MacLeish even in his more recent *J.B.*, dealing with Job in
much the same light as Frost did in *A Masque of Reason* fifteen
years earlier. In each case the land lies waste because man has
lost contact with the divine source of life, if indeed there
is one. Dwarfed by new knowledge of his history and of his
connection with nonhuman nature, Robinson's solitary man
on the horizon stands lone "against the glory of a world on
fire" where "Each must await alone at his own height/ Another

darkness or another light;". For all his modern knowledge, Robinson's man emerges from his pondering with no more than his ancestors' faith in ". . . an orient Word that will not be erased,/ Or, save in incommunicable gleams . . ./ Be found or known." *The Man Against the Sky* remains one of the great religious poems in English.

Robert Frost's *A Masque of Reason* and *A Masque of Mercy* both deal at length with questions of experience and spiritual faith. In the former, Job, after his death, with the questionable assistance of his shrewish wife, ponders with God the universal question why the good and devout person should suffer so much on earth. The God of Love and Mercy can only say that Job was God's appointed exemplar to "Establish once for all the principle/ There's no connection man can reason out/ Between his just deserts, and what he gets." In *A Masque of Mercy*, the flight of the Biblical Jonah from the wickedness of a modern metropolis emphasizes Frost's conviction that man will still have to seek the good individually, not in the mass, whether collectivist or democratic. Frost entitled an early poem "The Trial by Existence"; in this ordeal the most one can attain is "The mystic link to bind and hold/ Spirit to matter till death come." Frost's characters find the mystic link with the same inspired simplicity as of Silas, "the hired man," the migratory farm hand who daily did the best he could but dreamed of piling hay a little better; and who, old, poor, and dying, found home in "the place where, when you have to go there,/ They have to take you in."/ A farmer mending wall from stones in a stoneboat might find the immortal link in the fused clinker of a burned-out "star," its "spin" still eloquent to his hand of creative forces far beyond his world.

The revaluation of American democracy and history was another source of inspiration for this generation of poets. No genuine poet devoted his talents primarily to social causes; however, poems so emotionally and aesthetically lofty as Pound's *Hugh Selwyn Mauberley*, Eliot's *The Waste Land*, and MacLeish's *The Hamlet of A. MacLeish* were soon to probe the condition of the human soul when there is too evidently "something rotten" in the state. Beset by economic and social conflict and confronted by the rising tide of naturalistic and collectivist ideologies, many Americans continued to hold in mind Lincoln's query at Gettysburg: whether "a new nation conceived in liberty and dedicated to the proposition" of human equality "could long endure." Indeed, could the "simple, separate" individual exist on Whitman's democratic terms— "En-Masse"? Man had been dwarfed by science, and the machine; was he now to be engulfed and leveled by some flood of totalitarian mediocrity? The deep shadow of this doubt permeated Robinson's poems as a philosophical question; it motivated and tempered Frost's stubborn individualism.

Sandburg, however, believed in the people, the mass, as the alembic from which the great person would be distilled, as in the case of Lincoln, the liberator, of whom he wrote a great prose study. The son of Swedish immigrants well acquainted with privation, Sandburg himself was distilled from the mass in one generation; he gratefully embraced Jeffersonian idealism and the egalitarianism of Whitman, who influenced him profoundly. In his poetry, the grubby Fish Crier on a shabby street in Chicago gives back value received from a society he approves with his whole heart:

> His face is that of a man terribly glad to be selling fish,
> terribly glad that God made fish, and customers to whom
> he may call his wares from a pushcart.

His steelworker makes "Prayers of Steel"—he becomes the crowbar, the hammer, the spike—he prays: "Lay me on an anvil, O God./ Beat me and hammer me into a steel spike./ . . . Let me be the great nail holding a skyscraper together through blue nights into white stars." As fervidly as his confident love of the people Sandburg's satire flames out at abuses of power or privilege: for example, at the rich man on the lake front who fenced off the beach from "hungry men, and children looking for a place to play./ . . . As a fence it is a masterpiece./ . . . Passing through the bars and over the steel points will go nothing except Death, and the Rain, and Tomorrow."

His book-length poem, *The People, Yes,* is a vital bardic account of American democratic culture.

Stephen Vincent Benét was twenty years younger than Sandburg; his poetry was based on the traditional forms of English balladry and epic. Like Sandburg he found in American history an inspiration for his revaluations of American life, his fidelity to the Jeffersonian tradition. Like Sandburg he feared the authoritarian subversion of democracy either by a privileged class or by an ignorant rabble. His writings celebrate the American myth, the folklore of history, intensified by his satire of the materialistic enemies of democratic progress. Indeed, his early death at forty-five resulted in part from the overstrain of his zealous public life during the depression years, inspired by the consequent attacks on democracy and the rise of Hitler.

John Brown's Body, which first won Benét international attention, is the best American historical narrative in poetry—convincing in its characterization, impressive in its epical mastery of great events, and the lofty themes of toleration and freedom symbolized in the mythology of the Civil War by John Brown and Lincoln. If this was his *Iliad,* then *Western Star,* posthumously published, was his *Odyssey,* a picturesque fiction of the first British settlements, epitomizing historical events and people, emphasizing popular individualism, freedom and responsibility as early ingredients of a democracy fundamentally different from the European societies from which the colonists came:

> They tried to fit you with an English song
> And clip your speech into the English tale,
> But, even from the first, the words went wrong,
> The catbird pecked away the nightingale.

In his ballads, well-known, half-legendary figures of American life evoke the American frontier experiences responsible for certain traits of the character and behavior of Americans today. "The Ballad of William Sycamore," storied woodsman and scout, begins characteristically:

My father, he was a mountaineer,
His fist was a knotty hammer,
He was quick on his feet as a running deer,
And he spoke with a Yankee stammer.

And some are wrapped in the linen fine,
And some like a Godling's scion;
But I was cradled on twigs of pine
In the skin of a mountain lion.

Fundamentally, both Robinson and Frost were humanists, not reformers. They were interested in the individual, and in the situations that formed character or put it to the test. As New England traditionalists, they admired the qualities of independence, intellectual awareness, and responsibility—the compulsion to do one's best. Neither believed that these qualities were primarily associated with a given social class, but still, in the words of the old New England, "you don't make a silk purse of a sow's ear." Frost's characters are in the long tradition of the land—the farm, the woodlands, the small village— where Frost himself was farmer and schoolmaster most of his life until he went to England at the age of thirty-eight to find a publisher for his first book of poems. Like many humble New Englanders he had the opportunity for collegiate education; his friends and neighbors were intellectually alive, although in his poems one might be an apple grower, while another is a poor farm hand whose brother directs a bank. As for Robinson, from Maine, not Massachusetts, his father was a merchant. He grew up in a more sophisticated urban community than Frost and his characters are drawn principally from this environment. When he went to live in New York, he found that what he had learned of people in New England was equally true of people and life in the larger setting.

Robinson's most impressive poems are his book-length tragedies, such as *Matthias at the Door,* and the poems based upon the Arthurian romances. His people are prone to make the wrong choices: they succumb to irresponsible desire for power; or to greed, cowardice, and envy; or to the weak desire to command and control other lives; always seeking the materialistic instead of the spiritual goal. They hazard moral conviction against the odds of the market place, "where squandered men/ Drag ruins of half-warriors to the grave." These longer poems are complex in their psychological involvement and wit, but they compare in power with similar works of Browning. Hence they have had a more limited audience than his popular short sketches and character studies. Among these, "Ben Jonson Entertains a Man from Stratford" is a masterful study of Shakespeare, the great man unable to be content with the dimensions of his life and his own genius—greedy for more and more "height," while the spider, death, lurks to net him on the wing. As he tells Ben Jonson:

> "That's Nature, the kind mother of us all. . . .
> It's Nature, and it's Nothing. It's all Nothing.
> It's all a world where bugs and emperors
> Go singularly back to the same dust,
> Each in his time; and the old, ordered stars
> That sang together, Ben, will sing the same
> Old stave to-morrow."

The all-too-human greed for immortal power that Robinson discerned in Shakespeare was translated into the epic proportions of a civilization in *Merlin* (1917) and *Lancelot* (1920). These magnificent poems have the sweep of the Arthurian stories, and retain some fidelity to them, but they are also clear allegories of the spiritual failure of leadership on the eve of the First World War. The aging Merlin, Arthur's kingmaker and statesman, forsakes his duty to Arthur for the young love of Vivien, and returns too late to "a dying world" in which the passion of Lancelot and Queen Guinevere, the consequent intrigues and bloodshed of the rival knights, have left Arthur's civilization in ruins.

Tristram, which is independent from Robinson's Arthurian cycle, is one of the quite shattering verse tragedies, resolved either by regeneration or death, written in the poet's last decade. These also are foreshadowed in one or more of Robinson's brilliant short narratives. So Cavender, Nightingale, and Matthias, protagonists of great tragic poems, are to some degree epitomized in "Richard Cory," the village gentleman, whose perfections "fluttered pulses" if he but said "Good-morning" on his walk:

> And he was rich—yes, richer than a king—
> And admirably schooled in every grace:
> In fine, we thought that he was everything
> To make us wish that we were in his place.

> So on we worked, and waited for the light,
> And went without the meat, and cursed the bread;
> And Richard Cory, one calm summer night,
> Went home and put a bullet through his head.

Robinson has been called a cold poet, but greater discernment finds his passion the more moving because restrained, as indeed is also his wit, which like all great dramatic talents his own contains. In *Talifer*, Karen traps Dr. Quick by her phenomenal physical attractiveness, but he finds her a "cool brain" in disguise. "Like an ivory fish" she is "fascinating, but not proliferous, or domestic, and not good to eat." He is able to get rid of her only at Oxford, "where she'd had a fur-lined assignation with the past since her first sight of the Greek alphabet."

Robert Frost's poems are generally in small scale, but their apparent simplicity is deceptive. He calls himself "a synecdochist"; he gives the part for the whole, because it is the nature of poetry to "make you remember what you didn't know you knew." Most often this subtlety is a casually suggested connection between man and nature. In "The Axe-Helve," a humble country craftsman discusses the education of his children while showing the poet the perfect ax handle which he shaped by hand to the natural grain of the perfectly suitable hickory bough. The real poem, the "synecdoche," completed only in the reader's mind, is the shaping of nature by experience to form human character. As the craftsman said:

> He liked to have it slender as a whipstock,
> Free from the least knot, equal to the strain
> Of bending like a sword across the knee.

He showed me that the lines of a good helve
Were native to the grain before the knife
Expressed them, and its curves were no false curves
Put on it from without. And there its strength lay
For the hard work. He chafed its long white body
From end to end with his rough hand shut round it.

It is a poem on education but it is also a poem on art, for Frost once wrote that "art strips life to form."

So, deep in the forest a cord of wood, expertly cut and piled and long left to decay, is an enigma of human waste, until the sudden illumination of the last two lines (below) equates all energies—whether of man or of rotting wood—in the frugal economy of nature which man calls death:

I thought that only
Someone who lived in turning to fresh tasks
Could so forget his handiwork on which
He spent himself, the labor of his axe,
And leave it there far from a useful fireplace
To warm the frozen swamp as best it could
With the slow, smokeless burning of decay.

However much his lyrics may deal with nature, man is always Frost's genuine subject. In "Two Look at Two" the buck and his doe are beautiful indeed in the forest, but after forty lines the real poem occurs in the last two lines, when the animals look beyond the forest wall into the watching eyes of two human lovers:

As if the earth in one unlooked-for favor
Had made them certain earth returned their love.

As Frost has defined it, a poem "begins in delight and ends in wisdom" and it always provides at least "a momentary stay against confusion."

Such poems are always, to some degree, related to social themes, but often Frost's object is even more pointedly emphasized. "Mending Wall" is rooted in his knowledge of the ways of nature, "that doesn't love a wall,/ That wants it down!" But when the poem was published, in 1914, at the beginning of the World War, what could be more ominous than the farmer

> Bringing a stone grasped firmly by the top
> In each hand, like an old-stone savage armed

blindly repeating his father's saying:

> "Good fences make good neighbors."

This was indeed a poem dealing naturalistically with war. Yet more explicit is "Fire and Ice," written between the two wars:

> Some say the world will end in fire,
> Some say in ice.
> From what I've tasted of desire
> I hold with those who favor fire.
> But if it had to perish twice,
> I think I know enough of hate
> To say that for destruction ice
> Is also great
> And would suffice.

In a day when the world's survival depends upon mankind's choosing between two laws of nature

> the natural law of greed and hate,
> or the natural law of love

we may fittingly conclude our remarks with these poems, written by a poet who has read the book of nature wisely, and to the end.

MAXWELL GEISMAR

4: Society and the Novel

THE RISE of naturalism in the American novel was the dominant movement in American fiction from the early 1900's to the 1920's. It opened the road for everything that followed and it elevated American writing as a whole from a provincial native form to a world literature.

But literary movements never have the convenient chronologies that historians would prefer to see. The usual date given for the arrival of naturalism on the American scene is around 1910. Yet Theodore Dreiser, the pioneer of this movement, the true innovator and ancestor of modern American realism, published *Sister Carrie* as early as 1900. Frank Norris published *McTeague*—a highly realistic account of lower-middle-class American life—in 1899. Norris also published *The Octopus*, a novel about the California wheat farmers—and a predecessor of John Steinbeck's *The Grapes of Wrath*—in 1901.

Further still, let us note in passing that Stephen Crane wrote *Maggie: A Girl of the Streets*, in 1893, and *The Red Badge of Courage* in 1895, and—to add other figures to the ancestors of naturalism in our literature—it was Jack London who introduced the influence of Darwin and Nietzsche into genteel popular fiction in the early 1900's. London published two more notable books—*The Iron Heel*, in 1907, and *Martin Eden* in 1909—which were the products of the socialism which he loudly proclaimed, while he was still the most highly-paid popular fictioneer of the period. Oddly enough, too, it was the New York aristocrat, Edith Wharton—one of the "great ladies" of our literary annals—who did those early and brilliant satires of our new western wealth (even before *The Custom of the Country*, in 1913) which so influenced Sinclair Lewis that his best novel, *Babbitt*, was dedicated to her. These authors and these novels are part of the early history of the naturalistic or realistic movement in American fiction. The date of 1910, used generally to mark the advent of this movement, might better be regarded as the climax or culmination of its first phase. The real starting point of modern realism was in the early or mid-nineties, and its end was somewhere in the early 1940's. The whole cycle of the movement was about fifty years.

It should also be remembered that the American novelist William Dean Howells began to concentrate on the social injustices of finance-capitalism as early as the mid-1880's. The realism of Howells, mild as it was in certain areas, preceded the naturalism of London, Norris, and Dreiser, just as the realism of the 1920's and 1930's followed the hard core of the naturalistic movement, about which the later novelists themselves were often ignorant. But what was this "hard core" of American naturalism? It is easy enough to outline the principles of the movement. But it is very difficult to see these principles operating in the work of individual novelists except as a kind of rigid yardstick to evaluate each writer, and thereby to ignore—or to miss completely—the personal, temperamental and technical qualities which make each artist possess his own personal vision of life.

A novel is, after all, a work of art, not a scientific treatise. Unlike a philosophic "system," or a moral sermon, or a logical exposition, a novel is fluid, organic in nature, often shifting and ambiguous in content. Even the French novelists of the nineteenth century who formulated the principles of naturalism and influenced our own literature, hardly ever followed their own theories in their fiction—or became ridiculous when they did. It was Emile Zola who best formulated this code of a new "scientific literature" with the study of environment and heredity as its center: a literature which would "exclude the occult." Henceforth the "irrational" was out, and this new movement stressed the natural causes of those phenomena for which metaphysics had given only supernatural explanations. Its central purpose was to develop an experimental approach to human destiny in an impersonal, or amoral, universe.

These earlier European naturalists were also trying to cut through superstitions, prejudices, the layers of encrusted habit or custom which form the veneer—or the armored shell—of any civilization. The "materialism" of the new movement was a protest against the false use of spiritual values, or the use of spiritual values to inhibit rather than to enlarge the vision of mankind. The "determinism" which became the most vulnerable point of the naturalistic credo was the attempt to study social environment for the purpose of understanding its products. "Anatomists and physiologists, I feel you everywhere!" Sainte-Beuve exclaimed in his review of *Madame Bovary*, while to the French historian, Taine, all the vices and virtues of humanity were simply the products of chemical processes. What a wonderful *illusion* of science, indeed, was cherished by all these late-nineteenth-century thinkers and artists!—the same science which so far, in the mid-twentieth century, has found its supreme rationale in creating more and more devastating missiles of mass destruction.

The point is that Zola was actually a black romantic beneath all his "scientific" theories about naturalism, and Dreiser, for example, was influenced, not by Zola at all, but by Balzac—as Henry James was, at the other pole of our American fiction. The differences in the *practice* of naturalism between a Frank Norris, a Jack London, a Stephen Crane, or a Dreiser are just as great as the differences in temperament among all these writers. True, they all started with a common belief in a rather loosely defined idea of evolutionary scientific progress, but Jack London, for example, was another dark and possessed romantic spirit who was really far closer to Edgar Allan Poe than to his own colleagues. His vision of the world—Darwinesque and Nietzschean in essence—was rigid, harsh, sadistic, macabre, ironical, and ultimately suicidal. Dreiser's literary cosmos was, by contrast, brooding, tender, fluid. For all of Dreiser's stress on materialism and determinism—on the blind, savage forces of nature and man's helplessness; or on his famous "chemisms," a word he used for love—his best works are filled with a sense of the mystery and the divinity of life.

But Dreiser was a contradictory and complex figure. Like any major writer, he is not subject to quick and easy analysis. *Sister Carrie*, branded as "vulgar" or "immoral" in the early 1900's, was a touching little fable of a provincial farm girl and a Chicago saloonkeeper. Dreiser came from the humblest origins of the society he portrayed so acutely, so honestly. Part of the early opposition to his work no doubt stemmed from the fact that he represented the new immigrant strain in our culture which was threatening the refined and genteel Anglo-Saxon domination of the national letters. Another part of the protest against Dreiser's early novels was simply due to the fact that he dealt with low, commonplace and vulgar subjects—such as ordinary people. And while he dealt with such "sordid" material—that is to say, with the conditions of life which existed in the American scene of the 1900's—he stressed, relentlessly, the sexual elements of human nature which doubtless also persisted in the common life of America, if not in the upper reaches of its polite literature.

His second novel, *Jennie Gerhardt*, in 1911, was based on the illicit love affair of a wealthy businessman and another untutored and yet admirable heroine. (These early heroines of Dreiser's, incidentally, were based partly on the lives and careers of his own sisters.) This was the way American life really was. Yet curiously enough, of all our writers, Dreiser had the most "European" feeling of respect, admiration, and affection for women as women—a rare strain in our native literature. With *The Financier* and *The Titan*, in 1912 and 1914 respectively, he struck an altogether new note in his own career and in the annals of our writing. Here were studies of the new social structure of a finance-capitalism which was rapidly transforming the "mixed" society of town and farm—that innocent, provincial "country life" out of which Dreiser had come.

These first two novels of a projected trilogy were among the best of Dreiser's fictions, even though they are rather neglected in our own country. (*The Stoic*, the final novel of the trilogy, published posthumously in 1947, is less good.) Meanwhile, with *The "Genius,"* in 1915, he stirred up another great censorship battle in the national letters, and established a new area of sexual freedom which marked the real end of puritanism in our art. In the ten years between *The "Genius"* and *An American Tragedy*, in 1925, Dreiser poured out short stories, plays, essays, memoirs, and the first volume of his autobiography, *A Book About Myself*. The *American Tragedy* itself, generally considered Dreiser's greatest novel, was the tale of another western provincial hero—another small soul—caught up in the trap of wealth and "success." That was the dominant pattern of American society, as Dreiser saw it, and who was to blame when the novel's hero murdered the girl who had consoled him during his youth because she now stood in the way of a marriage into the best financial circles? Who *is* to blame, indeed, in the whole panorama of Dreiser's fiction, where poor, helpless human beings are always jostled and buffeted by the winds and tides of their own temperaments and passions; or by those larger cosmic or social forces which are so completely indifferent to individual need, or to individual suffering?

Dreiser's view of the universe was that of a turbulent dark whirlpool which sucked down the individual into its abysmal depths. Yet there was compassion in that "pessimism" of his. There was sympathy for the human plight, and tenderness for the victims of life—and often a kind of lyrical pagan admiration for all the beauties of existence, even in their violence, despite all their cruelty. Like Hawthorne, he had the tragic sense which only high artists have.

Meanwhile, he had opened the door for the later realists, from Sherwood Anderson and Ellen Glasgow to Sinclair Lewis. But with H. L. Mencken—the first great naturalistic philosopher of the 1920's—or so it seemed then—and with Sinclair Lewis, the realistic movement in modern American literature entered a new phase. The earlier naturalists, from Crane to Dreiser, had been somber in outlook. As in the work of Sherwood Anderson, or of the early Willa Cather, they proclaimed the inarticulate or barren suffering of the mainly western, ignorant, humble, and rural souls in the New World. To a certain degree, Lewis' first novels did this also. *Main Street*, the book which, in 1920, swept over our literary scene and galvanized the literature of revolt, was the story of a bleak western American town and a heroine who tried to reform it. This heroine was both romantic and inadequate; but at the time she became a kind of national symbol. The rebellious girl, Carol Kennicott, said Lewis, was the spirit "of that bewildered empire called the American Middlewest." Like Ibsen's Nora, she rattled the doll's house of American culture.

Two years later, *Babbitt*, probably Lewis' best work, gave to the world another new cultural type. Today we may understand that this famous novel was a nightmare vision—not so much realistic as surrealist in its basic conception—of the small American businessman in the completely standardized world of the future. *Babbitt* really belongs in the tradition of twentieth-century "antiutopian" fantasies from Aldous Huxley's *Brave New World* to George Orwell's *1984*. It is remarkable to see how completely Lewis projected himself into the future—or let us say, perhaps, the future-present. From the novel's inception in the hero's bedroom—"as neat and negative as a block of artificial ice"—to the conclusion of its latest and biggest real-estate deal, this book was a brilliant poetic vision of an altogether mass-minded society. It is our native Inferno of the mechanized hinterland, or the "ultimate in Rotary," where dwell a new race of synthetic and prefabricated human beings.

But George F. Babbitt was not happy in this world of prefabricated human relations; and the early Sinclair Lewis despised it. That is the point of the novel. Lewis gave a more sympathetic account of the "real" American businessman in the *Dodsworth* of 1929. Meanwhile he surveyed the field of scientific research in the *Arrowsmith* of 1925; and two years later, in *Elmer Gantry*, he took on the whole gamut of primitive and revivalist religion in the United States. In technique this was one of Lewis' less successful novels, yet beneath his sense of farce and comedy is his anger at any debasement of the human spirit, his moral outrage at any corruption of legitimate human values. There are sections of *Elmer Gantry* which suggest the best things in *Babbitt*, and again they possess a kind of surrealist and extra-satirical quality. In both these novels the note of compassion is matched by the element of a hard and biting social satire which played over all the foibles and follies of modern American life. Sinclair Lewis stripped the veils away from all our national illusions in the areas of business, religion, science, politics, social reform, even philanthropy. That was his literary purpose, and he fulfilled it well.

What area of American life in the 1920's was there, indeed, upon which Lewis (along with H. L. Mencken, or Ring Lardner) did *not* cast his jaundiced and critical eye, his stony reptilian gaze? In the great tradition of liberal American democracy—from Tom Paine and Thomas Jefferson, from Emerson, Thoreau, Melville, and Walt Whitman down to these writers of the 1920's—the major function of our literature has been to study the conditions of our natural and social existence—to shed over this the vision of our most talented individualists—and to express its conclusions with the utmost freedom. Ours has been mainly a literature of protest, of criticism, of revolt, and it will be a sad day for our culture and our art if our novelists should ever give up their most native and profound heritage.

But with this emphasis on a satiric rather than a tragic America in the twenties, both strains of the realistic movement flowed along concomitantly. In John Dos Passos' famous novels—the trilogy *U.S.A.*—and in William Faulkner's lurid dramas of the deep South, there were the fused elements of a deep moral conviction as to human justice and of a sharp satiric survey of American society. It was this group of later American fiction writers—including Ernest Hemingway, Scott Fitzgerald, and other members of the famous "Lost Generation"— who brought the naturalistic movement to its climax, and our native letters to the status of a world literature. They were high aesthetic individuals, these figures of the twenties, who represented the true peak and ending—rather than the beginning—as was thought then—of this movement in our literature, and who still today form the dominant image of American culture in world opinion.

Yet art oscillates always, as Otto Rank said, between the two poles of the community and the individual. In the sudden shock of the great depression during the 1930's, the whole drift of our literature turned again to the pressing problems of our social scene, and back toward the original purpose and meaning of the earlier naturalistic movement.

John Steinbeck, in another famous novel of the period, *The Grapes of Wrath* (1939), dramatized the plight of the "Okies," the western farmers who had lost their farms. There is no doubt that this is still a solid and durable novel, a key work of its period, and in some respects an epic chronicle of the depression years in our western agrarian culture. In another notable series of novels, the southern writer Thomas Wolfe described the face of the nation during the years of social strife: the promise and the reality of American life from his native hill country to the highest reaches of New York society, and back again to the slums of Brooklyn. Other novelists of the thirties, such as James T. Farrell, concentrated on studies of the poor and the dispossessed in the once-again tragic areas of our culture. Farrell's heavy, massive trilogy, *Studs Lonigan*, written from 1932 to 1935, still remains a notable work of its genre, while in turn such a novelist as Erskine Caldwell concentrated on the "poor whites" of our Southland. With such works the literary movement called naturalism had come full circle almost back to its original aims and purposes; and the movement as a whole could be called complete.

It was probably not a coincidence that the two new major literary voices in the United States of the 1940's—the late Richard Wright and Henry Miller—were both, in a sense, "underground writers." Wright spoke, at his best, for the American Negroes of the South, who had never found such a powerful and disenchanted voice in our literature before. Henry Miller, by contrast, carried forward the sexual revolution in our letters. The celebrated "revolt of the flesh" which, in the history of the naturalistic movement had assumed an importance equal to that of its social criticism, Miller indeed now extended to the point of a defiant and satiric sensuality which mocked at all our Anglo-Saxon and middle-class restraints and conventions, if not indeed at all the goals and values of modern society as a whole.

On a more conventional level, novelists like John O'Hara and James Gould Cozzens carried forward the naturalist technique and its sharp cutting-edge of social satire, just as John Hersey maintained the American literary conscience. Yet Wright and Miller were more powerful, authentic literary voices in themselves because they had instinctively chosen to be "subterranean writers." They marked the true ending of the great literary movement—call it naturalism, call it realism —which had lasted for half a century in American letters, which had done its work and left its mark. And perhaps, like the classic figures in the Greek myths, they also felt the need to go underground in order to find new sources of life, and new directions for their work.

At least one may hope that in some future "spring," in some further revival or renascence of American letters, in a brighter world than ours is now, the literary heirs and descendants of naturalism and realism will emerge from their Lethean retreat to deal once more with the real issues of their time, and to produce another series of novels as good as the best we have had under the aegis of this movement during the last fifty years.

ALAN S. DOWNER

5: The Revolt from Broadway

THE NEW movement in the drama begins in New York City, on Broadway, the theatrical center of the United States. The last week of July, 1916, regular playgoers were invited to see *The Heart of Wetona*, a melodrama about a white man's love for an American Indian woman; or *Common Clay*, a sentimentalized problem play; or *Beau Brummel*, a costume romance of the early nineteenth century in England; or *Just a Woman*, a farrago of domesticity. Half a century after Ibsen and Strindberg, and several decades after Chekhov and Hauptmann and the reformers of the Continental theatres and their repertories, theatre in the United States was still tied to the dramatic forms and conventional attitudes of the past. A wholly commercial operation, it insisted that its function was to entertain, and it defined entertainment as escapism.

During these same weeks, four hundred miles north-north-east of New York City, in a little fishing village on the tip of Cape Cod, a group of artists of many sorts—painters, sculptors, poets, novelists—drawn together by the enthusiasm of George Cram Cook, organized themselves into a theatrical group named the Provincetown Players. They rented a fishing shack at the end of a pier reaching out into the Atlantic Ocean, a small building capable of seating fewer than a hundred people, built

42

a makeshift stage, and there produced a one-act play called *Bound East for Cardiff*.

It is a simple play, totally unlike anything that could have been seen at that time in New York City. Its brief action consists of the dialogue between a dying sailor and his buddy who tries to cheer him up. The sailor has been injured in an accident on board a freighter, and he lies in his bunk dreaming of the green fields of the farm that he longed to settle down on, leaving the life of the sea forever. The other sailors, a sampling of the races of the world, quarrel and argue and joke in their miserable, cramped quarters. They do not understand each other and the dying man cannot communicate with them since he represents the loneliness of the individual in the world. The average theatregoer of the time would hardly recognize *Bound East for Cardiff* as a play at all; it has no action, no violence, no romance. It is little more than a mood, or a perceptive comment on experience. But its immediate success with audiences at the Provincetown Theatre gave courage to the group to carry on their work, and inspired its author to write a series of plays which marked the coming of age of the theatre in America and established him as the first American playwright to achieve stature in the world theatre. His name was Eugene O'Neill.

As I have suggested, the coming of age of the theatre in the United States was late in contrast to the new-theatre movements of the continent of Europe. It was also late in relation to the maturing of the American novel and American poetry. The professional theatre is always a more conventional art than its counterparts in literature and the fine arts. This is not because it is lacking in inspiration or has a distaste for new ideas but because the theatre itself is a large and complex medium. Not one creator, the author, but many—directors, actors, designers, even costumers—are involved in creating the final product. Involved also is the playing place, usually a substantial building with permanent and expensive equipment. Experimentation is difficult and indeed fruitless unless this complex of individuals and physical plant can be given some kind of unity either of idea or of practice. That is why it is necessary to create an organization like the Provincetown Players, or the Washington Square Players, which began almost at the same time in Greenwich Village, New York City, before a revolution in play production or playwrighting can bear fruit.

Actually, the American commercial theatre, toward the end of the nineteenth century, had made some timid gestures toward reforming its sentimentality and tendencies to melodrama. James A. Herne experimented with naturalism in plays like *Shore Acres* and *Margaret Fleming,* supported and encouraged by the naturalistic novelists and critics of the time. Early in the twentieth century, Percy MacKaye and William Vaughn Moody attempted to revive fantasy and poetic drama, and Moody's *The Great Divide* managed to achieve some success.

The theatre in the United States, like the nineteenth-century theatre generally, was a realistic theatre, and the first signs of its coming of age are to be found in the attempt of playwrights to treat important subjects or ideas as realistically as they had hitherto treated settings and characterization. Unfortunately the theatre operators, the producers, were content with surface realism, with the illusion of reality, and cared little about reality of idea. So American theatre audiences had to be content with the sentimental melodramas of playwrights like David Belasco, produced with almost fanatic attention to the minutiae of realistic illusion. The appearance of realism, what O'Neill was to call the banality of surfaces, persuaded audiences to accept in the theatre subjects and themes treated in ways that would have provoked scornful laughter in any novel that pretended to equally serious stature. After Eugene O'Neill the American theatre could never return to the past.

O'Neill was not produced by spontaneous combustion. Behind him lay the skill and craftsmanship developed by the various artists of the nineteenth-century theatre; a large body of gifted actors; the revolutionary ideas of such nondramatic writers as Karl Marx, Sigmund Freud, and Friedrich Nietzsche; the programs of various American universities and colleges which attempted to liberate the minds of young playwrights by exposing them to the best that had been thought and said in the world, plus the inspiration of the Provincetown group. O'Neill came from a distinguished nineteenth-century theatrical family, had read widely among the advanced thinkers of the progressive movements of the nineteenth century, had studied at Princeton and at Harvard, and had found his first audience with the Provincetown group.

It is perhaps necessary to insist on the native influences that brought about the revolution in American drama. In spite of the success of the new theatre in Europe, the European repertory did not exert a very powerful influence on American writers. Ibsen, while read and occasionally produced, was never much to American taste, perhaps because his great theme, his insistence on the rights of men to shake off the shackles of the past—what Shaw calls his iconoclasm—had been written into the Declaration of Independence and the American Constitution half a century before Ibsen, and could hardly create the shock of novelty and revelation that it did in nations and cultures organized on different principles.

Those leaders of the European theatre who did exert some influence on American writing and production seem to be three: first, a Swede, August Strindberg, whose streamlined, direct, and symbolic plays suggested to American writers that, even within the confines of the realistic theatre, drama of power and significance was a possibility; second, Georg Kaiser and the German expressionists, who demonstrated techniques which permitted the creation of a kind of subjective play of great appeal to a generation which was looking more and more deeply into itself (it should be pointed out that though expressionism as a form was never successful in the United States, many of the techniques of the expressionistic writers have been taken over and utilized with freedom and success); third, such producers and directors as Jacques Copeau, whose fresh and vital and simplified approach to the staging of plays, widely seen and reported on by American travelers, encouraged reforms in production to accompany the reforms in playwriting.

But it is not too strong to say that the reform of the American theatre depended ultimately on Eugene O'Neill and what his talent was to produce in the years between 1916 and 1926. O'Neill's contribution was threefold: he wrote plays that were highly original in form, indebted to but not imitative of the whole repertory of world theatre; he devised or assisted in devising unique methods of staging, carefully adjusted to the demands of each new play; he reflected in subject matter and theme not the contrived world of the theatre, or some conventional world of the past, but the life and thinking of his own time. And out of his craftsmanship and courage in creating and perceiving came a whole new repertory for the theatre in the United States.

O'Neill, although he was of Irish descent, could never be mistaken for anything but an American playwright. His characters are American: farmers, sailors, soldiers, businessmen and peddlers, common men and women. These had been the almost exclusive concern of the American theatre since its beginning, but O'Neill sees them in the light of postwar experience, not as theatrical stereotypes. His farmers are hard-bitten, violent New Englanders fighting the soil, not happy peasants rejoicing in a kind of Garden of Eden. His sailors are the ragged crews of freighters, not the spanking jack-tars of patriotic musical comedy. His drunkards do not reform to provide a moral lesson for the audience, and his love affairs end in Strindbergian catastrophe rather than the laced valentines of domestic sentimentality. His situations, too, are American: he writes of the heirs of New England puritanism, of the Civil War, of the artist's life in Greenwich Village, and one of his few historical characters is Marco Polo, the first traveling salesman.

But his treatment of both characters and situations is always in terms of twentieth-century thought. Take, for example, his Civil War play, *Mourning Becomes Electra*. The Civil War had always been a much-used subject in the popular theatre, almost from the moment that it started. But the popular treatment usually involved a northern officer who found himself in love with a daughter of the Confederacy. For O'Neill the Civil War is merely a background for a story of family guilt and expiation, based ostensibly on the great *Oresteia* trilogy by Aeschylus, but owing much more, in terms of both power and tragic tension, to the discoveries of Freudian and Jungian psychology. Or look at his play about American farm life, *Desire Under the Elms*. In popular drama the kindly old New England farmer always found himself under the necessity of going to the big city to rescue his son who had fallen upon evil ways. O'Neill's farmer is ruthless, possessive, and Bible-ridden; his son is in open revolt against him, and he refuses to raise a hand to help him when he becomes trapped in a murder charge.

These plays are not important or revolutionary simply because they emphasize the grim and unpleasant aspects of American life. They are important and revolutionary because for the first time in the American theatre they reflect the postwar world, the world in which most certainties—moral, ethical, and to an extent legal—had given way to uncertainties. It was no longer possible to say with assurance what action was right and what was wrong. All actions had to be freshly examined, all positions freshly argued, all characters and situations freshly analyzed, in the attempt to establish new values and new certainties for the 1920's. O'Neill achieved these things with enormous theatrical skill, and great creative power. It was his experimentalism and his success that encouraged the whole crowd of new playwrights—Maxwell Anderson, Philip Barry, Thornton Wilder, Elmer Rice, and Robert E. Sherwood—who came into the theatre after O'Neill had shown the way.

The identifying characteristic of the American theatre after 1916 is its relentless experimentalism. The work of each major playwright turns from one form to another, one mode or attitude to another, from the well-made play to the loose panorama, from realism to symbolism to expressionism; or the playwright will invent his own combination of forms and modes. Experiment in playwrighting is accompanied by experiment in acting techniques, in design, direction, and lighting. But, because all was kept within the control of the practical theatre, because all was done with the sole purpose of translating the author's vision into a dramatic experience, the audience—which might be expected to reject the unconventional—soon came to welcome and encourage it.

Since any American playwright with more than two plays to his credit will exhibit experimental tendencies, it will be necessary to select a few who exemplify different kinds of experiment in the twenties and thirties. Maxwell Anderson, Philip Barry, and Thornton Wilder have been chosen because they all write about contemporary American society, the standard subject of the well-made realistic play, and because they move in sharply differing directions from the conventional form and mode.

Although he began as a journalist and a poet, Maxwell Anderson achieved his first wide success with a series of prose plays painstaking in their realism. The characters are like photographs from life; the language reproduces with fidelity the class and circumstances of the characters. The central issue of the action, more often than not, is a problem of concern to the immediate audience. *What Price Glory* (written in collaboration with Laurence Stallings) with its burly, brawling, foul-mouthed protagonists, its disillusioned portrait of men at war, reflected the growing realization that war was not fought according to romantic or genteel notions which had prevailed, but that it was tough, profane—and yet not without humor. *Gods of the Lightning* (written in collaboration with Harold Hickerson) was a play of social protest based on the questions raised by the actual trial of two anarchists. *Both Your Houses* was a satire on the members of the Federal legislature. The early postwar period, during which these plays were written, was marked by a critical and satirical mood—and the success of the plays was as much due to the immediacy of their subjects as to the skill of their writing.

But Anderson was restless under the restrictions of what might be called journalistic playwrighting. With Bernard Shaw, he believed that the theatre is "essentially a cathedral of the spirit, devoted to the exaltation of men," and with Goethe that "dramatic poetry is man's greatest achievement on his earth." Determined "to reach into the upper air of poetic tragedy," he put aside his success in prose realism and wrote *Elizabeth the Queen*. If this was a bold step, it was only half a step toward true experimentation. The play is historical in subject matter and the verse is basically iambic pentameter, both elements being the conventional ones for poetic drama in English.

The success of *Elizabeth* encouraged Anderson to take the giant step of writing a verse tragedy which was distinctively American and representative of the twentieth century. *Winterset* begins with the same materials as *Gods of the Lightning*, but it is less concerned with an apparent miscarriage of justice in a particular case than with the nature of justice itself. The characters are not drawn, as is conventional, from myth or legend; they are drawn from the American lower classes: the children of immigrants, vagabonds, workers, gangsters. This, of course, presented a problem of verisimilitude in creating a poetic vocabulary for types that are normally portrayed as inarticulate; Anderson solves the problem with some success by introducing characters who might be expected to have a rich heritage of literature and philosophy, like a Jewish rabbi. He also borrows much of his action from the more familiar plays of Shakespeare (his young lovers meet at a street dance [*Romeo*]; a mad judge conducts a trial in a thunderstorm [*Lear*]) and the analogy, which is never made explicit, inevitably gives added dimension, added stature to both the characters and the situations in which they are involved.

There have been many efforts to revive the ancient art of verse drama in the English language; *Winterset*, although it has some shortcomings particularly in the language, is almost the only play which has stayed within the limits of the practical theatre while achieving the elevation and universality to which all dramatic poets aspire. It is not closet drama, it is not eccentric, yet in its own way it forces actor, designer, and director to summon all the resources of their respective crafts to give the fullest realization to Anderson's script.

For example, few of the original spectators will ever forget the poetic skill with which the designer, Jo Mielziner, translated Anderson's initial stage direction into actuality. "The scene," the author wrote, "is the bank of a river under a bridgehead." What the rising curtain revealed was a dingy public street, framed at one side by a square, heavy tenement with a cellar entrance, but at the back, over it all, and arching away into the hidden distance, was the dominating and graceful span of an enormous bridge. The setting told the audience in advance that this small, earthbound action had dimensions beyond the recognition of the characters, that the action in the city street reached up and out into eternal truth.

So, too, with the actors: they were familiar, for the most part, through their appearances in motion pictures, where they had played the stereotyped young lovers and gangsters of melodrama. Without repeating the stereotype, or abandoning it, they used it as a basis for the creation of characters that assumed the validity of myth, the known and familiar projected into the unknowable and the unfamiliar. Thus Eduardo Cianelli, with the sharply-cut top coat, black felt hat, thin-lipped speech, and ever-ready revolver was enlarged into the abstract force of evil, the fascistic power outside the law of man or nations; the melodramatic villain became a spiritual force. So, too, Burgess Meredith, the wistful youth of Hollywood, became the image of a lost generation, orphaned not only in family, but in society. *Winterset*, as a play and as a performance, became one of the memorable achievements of the American theatre.

Like Anderson, Philip Barry began his career in what might be called the conventional theatre. Anderson's first successes were with the realistic, social plays; Barry first triumphed in the comedy of manners. Like many others of his generation, he was a product of George Pierce Baker's famous course in play-wrighting, the 47 Workshop, and he came from Harvard to Broadway equipped with impeccable taste, a sure sense of style, and a mildly ironic attitude toward the values of the social order. In a series of comedies, *Paris Bound, Holiday, The Animal Kingdom*, he depicted that society with a caressing and devastating hand, examining the undermining of the social contract by such forces as divorce and the business code, and making a strong plea for the dignity of the individual. The atmosphere of these plays is gay, the characters full of charm, the dialogue witty and pointed; the author's sense of his own time is so pervasive that the audience often felt that it was watching a cast tap-dancing on the edge of a volcano.

It was Barry's awareness of his society that occasionally drove him from the writing of comedies of manners to what must be called, for lack of a more precise term, fantasies, although there is nothing in them of the atmosphere of fairyland. In *Hotel Universe* (1930) he assembles a set of the characters familiar through the novels of F. Scott Fitzgerald in a typical playground of the bored rich, a Mediterranean villa. There is a suggestion of secondary meaning in the setting, a triangular terrace against a backdrop of sea and sky, "like a wedge in space," swept by the beam of a neighboring lighthouse, as one of the characters says, "like the Finger of God." Typically, some of the guests are drawn into a parlor game of charades, in which they burlesque the pomposity and business acumen of one of their number. The game is prophetic, for on the almost unlocalized platform, suspended in time and space, the characters proceed to cross and recross the boundaries of present and past, acting out their delusions and dreams, and finally arriving at ultimate realities. Heretofore, Barry had demanded of his actors only the polished skill of social comedians; now they were required to develop powers of impersonation in depth and breadth.

Here Come the Clowns (1938) made even greater demands, since it required a group of music hall artists not merely to perform their specialties but to enact pathetic, even tragic, situations. The story is a kind of allegory of good and evil in which each of the characters is driven to reveal his innermost thoughts by an "illusionist," though under his spell their revelations are all of pain and frustration: a midget, successful on the stage, living in both shame and terror lest he see his normal son off stage; a ventriloquist whose dummy speaks the thoughts he would not put into words; a stagehand searching for a theatre manager who has mysteriously disappeared. This is a highly original play, a warm and pitying dramatization of the plight of the common man in a society without a moral rudder; it is one of the few plays of the contemporary commercial theatre to deal directly with a theological issue; and it came from the pen of a man who set out to be an amused observer of the fads and foibles of idle, cultured hedonists.

Unlike Anderson and Barry with their beginnings in the conventional theatre, Thornton Wilder announced himself at once as an experimenter. The audience that entered the theatre at the first performance of *Our Town* (1938) found itself facing a curtainless, sceneryless stage. The beginning of the play was marked by the entrance of the Stage Manager, who lighted his pipe, cocked his hat over his eyes, and sat down to chat informally with the spectators about the play they were going to see. If the audience was at first startled by the novelty, they were soon able to adjust to it, and, through the necessarily sharpened focus on the actors, found themselves engrossed by a story so simple and commonplace that in other hands and under other conditions of production they might never have noticed it at all. The play is without the conflicts and tensions that are normally considered dramatic or theatrical: a young girl grows up, marries and dies in a New England village so isolated from the burning issues of the greater world that they are never hinted at. And yet this very isolation, emphasized by the bareness of the stage, brought to vivid life the problems, the conditions, the situation of everyman, so that this little play, seemingly so American in its frame of reference and its attitudes, has found an instant and continuing response in the hearts and minds of world audiences.

The Skin of Our Teeth (1942) is in many ways Wilder's most creative use of the theatre. His theme is the survival of the human race in the face of ignorance, catastrophe, and folly, and he moves backward and forward in time with a rapidity that reminds some critics of the *Finnegans Wake* of James Joyce. The play opens in the typical fashion of Victorian farce with a soliloquy by a pert chambermaid, but before long the walls of the room are leaning at crazy angles, Homer and the Muses and a baby mammoth are seeking shelter from the approaching icecap, the audience is urged to contribute its chairs to a fire to preserve the race from refrigeration. The free form of the play admits a convention of mammals at Atlantic City, the transformation of the chambermaid into Lilith and a camp follower in the Ultimate War, and a pageant of the great philosophers. For sheer variety and mingling of emotions, *The Skin of Our Teeth* approaches most closely a musical comedy, but its theme is a celebration rather than a mere exhibition of humanity. Wilder's use of familiar materials and conventions in a fresh way comes very close to that creative, poetic theatre toward which O'Neill urged his fellow workers to aspire.

All of the playwrights we have been considering first came to public attention between 1916 and 1930 and made major contributions to the coming of age of the American drama. They had many talented fellow workers—Robert Sherwood, with his sensitive response to the world-political situation, Sidney Howard, with his probing of social concepts—and they made way in the 1930's for playwrights like Clifford Odets and Sidney Kingsley, who reflected on the stage the stresses of the depression years. O'Neill and his followers set a high standard for American drama and sounded a call for writers with imagination, vitality, and technical skill. Like all the arts, the drama is seldom at its best for long, yet the impulse that came to the American theatre in the twenties has reasserted itself in the following decades, in the proletarian drama of the thirties, in the brisk satirical comedies of George S. Kaufman and various collaborators, leading to the emergence after World War II of the probing poetical tragedies of Arthur Miller and Tennessee Williams. But these are of a later day, and for another chapter in this book.

WALTER BLAIR

6: The Urbanization of Humor

IN NO OTHER type of contemporary American writing are the changes in American society during the early years of the century more apparent than in our humor. Our chief humorists until the 1920's were all rustic or western. Since the 1920's, by contrast, our famous humorists have been urban.

Created by Benjamin Franklin early in the eighteenth century, Poor Richard Saunders led a procession of prodigiously popular humorous characters who, for two centuries, delighted nationwide audiences and often even shaped political decisions. Poor Richard had the essential traits of these characters. He was a countryman, and the best-loved humorous pundits showed by their dialect and their subject matter their farm or frontier origins. Poor Richard was uneducated but so acute and so experienced in the ways of the world that he could make witty comments which a nation worshiping what it called "horse sense" vastly appreciated. So it was with later vernacular humorists. There were Davy Crockett, coonskin frontier congressman, and Lowell's Yankee farmer Hosea Biglow, who his creator said personified "common-sense vivified and heated by conscience." There was H. W. Shaw's Ohio bumpkin, Josh Billings, whose creed was, "You have got to be wize [he spelled it with a z] before you can be witty." There was Mark Twain, creator of the Missouri ragamuffin

Huck Finn and of the Connecticut Yankee, Hank Morgan—both, as Mark said, "ignoramuses" so far as book learning was concerned, but both so blessed with gumption that they could commune shrewdly.

The last giant in this procession of homespun humorists was Will Rogers, Oklahoma-born cowboy. "I've been eatin' pretty regular," said Will, "and the reason . . . is because I've stayed an old country boy." Thanks to varied media—syndicated newspaper columns, moving pictures, the radio—Will became more widely known than any of his predecessors in the tradition. But with his death in 1935—a symbolically appropriate one in an airplane crash—the procession ended. Since then some old-time humorists have won some prominence. An exceptional Harry Golden, aided by the timeliness of many of his preachments, could score a remarkable success—three best-selling books of humorous commentaries in a row. Nevertheless, during the quarter century since Rogers' death, no humorist of his type with an iota of his prominence has arisen.

During his last years, Rogers was actually an anachronism who offered proof that old humorous traditions die hard. Widespread education had led many Americans to believe that book learning, which old-time humorists had scorned, was a better guide to wisdom than horse sense. The incongruity between ignorance and insight, our oldest joke, was no longer sure-fire. The rural and frontier civilizations which had nurtured dialect humorists were being replaced by an urban civilization lacking respect for men who talk in the vernacular. Already, humor of a new and very different sort was burgeoning.

The magazine which would be largely responsible for the rise of this new humor, even before its start in 1925, disavowed interest in rural and small-town readers so important as part of the humorists' audience in the past:

THE NEW YORKER [said the Prospectus] will be the magazine which is not edited for the old lady in Dubuque. It will not be concerned in what she is thinking about. . . . THE NEW YORKER is a magazine avowedly published for a metropolitan audience and thereby will escape an influence which hampers most national publications. It expects a considerable national circulation, but this will come from persons who have a metropolitan interest.

Harold Ross, the author of the Prospectus, as editor, dominated the course of *The New Yorker*—the only important American humorous magazine since 1939—until his death in 1951. Not surprisingly, therefore, the announcement accurately forecast the magazine's history. And not surprisingly, *The New Yorker* attracted and sponsored four outstanding modern humorists, all with a distinctly urban flavor.

Clarence Shepard Day (1874-1935), Robert Benchley (1889-1945), James T. Thurber (1894-1961), and Sidney Joseph Perelman (1904-   ), all rose to prominence in the 1920's and are still appreciatively read. And though they did not entirely break with the past—no humorist does this—they did write humor based upon assumptions and emphasized techniques quite different from those of older humorists. They also employed new techniques.

Day, the son of a Wall Street broker, worked in the Stock Exchange after graduating from Yale, served in the U. S. Navy during the Spanish-American War, then became a journalist and a writer of sketches, essays, and books. Not, however, until he wrote a series of family reminiscences for *The New Yorker* and other magazines did he find his best and most popular vein. *God and My Father*, *Life with Father*, and *Life with Mother* (1932, 1935, 1937) were best sellers; a dramatization based upon them had a record run as a play and reincarnation as a successful motion picture.

Father, as Day pictured him, could have been an old-fashioned horse-sense philosopher if he had had a rural upbringing and had learned to say wise things in a witty way. Like Poor Richard, he has arrived at firm opinions about what is right on the basis of keen thinking and experience. He courageously takes stands and announces them. He is irked by those who carry on "all the chuckle-headed talk and rascality in business and politics":

He was always getting indignant about them, and demanding that they be stamped out. . . . And twice a day, regularly, he would have a collision, or bout, with the newspaper; it was hard to see why God had made so many damned fools. . . . I would try to persuade him . . . to accept the world as it was and adapt himself to it, since he could scarcely expect to . . . change the whole earth single-handed. Father listened to this talk with suspicion. . . .

God Himself does not awe this rugged individualist: "he seemed to envisage a God in his own image. A God who had small use for emotionalism and who prized strength and dignity. . . . Father and God . . . usually saw eye to eye."

Father's resemblance to ancient rustic oracles is obvious. But his depicter's tone contrasts sharply with that of nineteenth-century authors picturing similar characters. The earlier authors—a Mark Twain picturing a Huck Finn, let us say—admired such characters and shared their attitudes. Day, though fond of Father, regards him as a quaint figure of a bygone era; he questions his standards, laughs at his judgments, satirizes his outmoded ways. In most stories, Father's "antagonists" are an irresponsible, flutter-brained family. They don't know what they're doing; they bumble and blunder. But Father fails to get what he wants; the family flounders to triumph. Mother in particular, conniving, not overly careful with truth, unsystematic, amoral, constantly outwits him. The contrast is particularly clear in one story in which an old Yankee trick is assigned to Mother as she fights a battle in the continuous war with Father about household accounts. The old-time Yankee cheated his victim because he was shrewd enough to devise the trick. Mother, on the contrary, manages to get away with the operation because she is illogical enough to stumble upon this way of outwitting her spouse. And Day leaves no doubt that he prefers Mother's way of doing things.

Benchley, Thurber and Perelman, all like Day, depict different characters but similarly rebel against ancient standards. The nineteenth-century humorous ancestors of this trio, significantly, were foils for the horse-sensible characters. They were the simpletons, the characters who took the wrong

attitudes. Hosea Biglow's foil, for instance, was Birdofredum
Sawin, a stupid rascal who was taken in by the wartime fan-
fare which Hosea scornfully attacked. Mark Twain had a good
name for this group—"Inspired Idiots." Others called them
"literary comedians." They were as invariably wrong about
current problems as horse-sensible characters were right.

"The literary comedians," says Bernard De Voto, "presented
themselves as Perfect Fools, whereas our [modern] comedians
present themselves as Perfect Neurotics. There is no other difference." This may be true; but the difference is revolutionary.

Robert Benchley was an important contributor to *The New
Yorker,* to other magazines and newspapers, to the profits of
publishers of his collected pieces in fifteen books, and even to
those of moving picture companies which filmed nearly fifty
"shorts" in which he delivered monologues. In Benchley's very
popular writings, and as a movie actor, he constantly assumed
the role of a "Perfect Neurotic." The character he pretends
to be is prevented from doing harmless things he'd like to do
—leave a party when he wants, smoke a cigarette, wear a white
suit, pick flowers, and so on. The frustrations have given this
character phobias and complexes which he shows at work.
A reader is not surprised to find this assumed character ticking
off the symptoms of dementia praecox and finding that he
has all of them.

"Some of this," writes Benchley's son, "was exaggerated, but
not as much as might be supposed. Benchley was a highly subjective writer, and most of what he wrote was conditioned by
his feelings about himself." This modern humorist, then, exaggerates—as did old-time humorists. But whereas the oldsters
exaggerated the difficulties which they had to overcome and
their ability to cope with them, Benchley exaggerates the small-
ness of his difficulties and his inability to cope with them. And
the author's own troubles are like those of his comic character. J. Bryant III subtitles his profile of the humorist "A Study
in Professional Frustration," and indicates that Benchley's conception of himself is of a man constantly humiliated and defeated by trifles: ". . . he sees himself . . . not [as] the master
of high comedy, but the victim of low tragedy. King Lear loses

a throne; Benchley loses a filling. Romeo breaks his heart; Benchley breaks his shoelace. They are annihilated: he is humiliated. And to his humiliations there is no end." Benchley's humor constantly makes use of such humiliations and the assumed character's failure to handle trifling problems. He speaks of working in "the dementia praecox field." Bryant notices that "Every page of his books is riddled with . . . pitfalls for sanity. Madness so dominates the landscape of his humor that a second reading is necessary to recognize its other features."

Milder, temporary, or even violent and permanent aberrations had been far from unusual in the older humor. Many literary comedians made people laugh at their "inspired idiocy." But the difference between the assumed character and the character of his creator was an important incongruity. James Russell Lowell played up the differences between himself— sane, logical, sound in his attitudes—and Birdofredum Sawin— mildly mad, illogical, unsound in his attitudes. The contrast made for irony, and the irony often made for satire. Just as Clemens stood apart from his wrong-headed Pap Finn while Pap lauded racial discrimination, and thereby attacked an attitude which Clemens abhorred, many literary comedians made the "I" in their writings obviously, comically, and satirically different from his creator.

The new emphasis was not on differences but on resemblances. Benchley exaggerates what he believes are his own qualities. And the expectation is that instead of feeling superior to the comic character, the reader will identify with that character, and sympathize with him. "The fellow," he'll say, "suffers from much the same frustrations, the same fears, the same incompetency I suffer from." He'll join the assumed character in being irritated by all the self-confident people he encounters: efficiency experts, go-getters, club women, scientists—all those well-adjusted (and quite probably self-deceived) clods. Clarence Day's Father is a character who definitely belongs to the enemy forces; Benchley would align himself with Mother.

James T. Thurber worked on several newspapers before beginning, in 1927, an association with *The New Yorker* that continued till his death. He published several popular books and invaded Broadway and the movies.

Thurber's discussion of the nature of humor shows immediately his kinship with Benchley:

The things we laugh at are awful while they are going on, but get funny when we look back. And other people laugh because they've been through it too. . . . I think humor is the best that lies closest to the familiar, to that part of the familiar which is humiliating, distressing, even tragic. Humor is a kind of emotional chaos told about calmly and quietly in retrospect. There is always a laugh in the utterly familiar. . . . People can laugh out of a kind of mellowed self-pity as well as out of superiority.

The humiliation, the emotional chaos, are reminiscent of the misadventures of the "I" in Benchley's pieces. The identification of the reader with the suffering character is specific. Thurber adds that the events are "told about calmly and quietly in retrospect"—a shrewd comment which also applies to Benchley's way of telling about his emotional experiences.

A fine illustration is a portion of Thurber's story of what happened in Columbus, Ohio, the day the dam broke:

The only possible means of escape for us was to flee the house, a step which grandfather sternly forbade, brandishing his old army sabre in his hand. "Let the sons————come!" he roared. Meanwhile hundreds of people were streaming by our house in wild panic, screaming, "Go east! Go east!" We had to stun grandfather with the ironing board. Impeded as we were by the inert form of the old gentleman—he was taller than six feet and weighed almost a hundred and seventy pounds—we were passed, in the first half mile, by practically everybody else in the city. Had grandfather not come to, at the corner of Parsons Avenue and Town Street, we would unquestionably have been overtaken and engulfed by the roaring waters—that is, if there had *been* any roaring waters.

Quel dommage! But what calm, what quietude the author manifests in writing about the events! There is no mention of the narrator's attitude: with Hemingwayesque restraint, he writes not about the emotion but the happenings which produce the emotion. An important disparity is that between the harrowing happenings and the objectivity which marks their description.

The fact that this is a passage in what playfully purports to be an autobiography, *My Life and Hard Times,* at least based upon personal experiences, suggests that Thurber, like Benchley, tends to identify himself in essential ways with his first-person narrator. And the author's description of "humorists" shows that they qualify to write Thurberian humor by living as their characters also live:

They lead . . . an existence of jumpiness and apprehension. . . . [They] have a genius for getting into minor difficulties: they walk into the wrong apartments, they drink furniture polish for stomach bitters, they drive their cars into the prize tulip beds of haughty neighbors. . . .

Such a writer moves restlessly wherever he goes, ready to get the hell out at the drop of a pie-pan or the lift of a skirt. His gestures are the ludicrous reflexes of the maladjusted; his repose is the momentary inertia of the nonplussed. . . . He talks largely about small matters and smally about great affairs.

This characterizes "the humorist"; it also characterizes the protagonists in Thurber's pieces and their adventures. In his guise of pictorial artist, Thurber portrays similar characters: his men "are frustrated, fugitive beings; at times they seem vaguely striving to get out of something without being seen (a room, a situation, a state of mind), at other times they are merely perplexed and too humble or meek to move." Like Benchley's character, they are baffled both by people and by inanimate objects.

Benchley testifies to S. J. Perelman's leadership in "the dementia praecox field." Perelman, another *New Yorker* star, has pictured his alter ego in a guise much like those of Benchley and Thurber: he too is frustrated and put upon; he too is helpless in a hostile world. Even more than they he is victimized by free association: "The color drained from my face, entered the auricle, shot up the escalator, and issued from the ladies' and misses' section into the housewares department," he reports.

His assumed character's distinctions are two: First, he tries to swagger, to brazen things out. A man of less than ordinary presence, he deceives himself into believing that he's a handsome dog. "I am a fairly typical Yankee," he modestly asserts, "who looks like Gary Cooper, sings like Frank Sinatra and dances like Fred Astaire . . ." He describes himself as "this man, who by sheer poise and magnetism had surmounted the handicap of almost ethereal beauty. . . ." A man of limited intelligence, he tries to impress one with his learning. He dots his pages with showy French, German and Italian phrases, with exotic names for clothing or strange dishes.

Second, the character he assumes has been brain-washed by mass media. He believes advertisements concocted by Madison Avenue slickers. He accepts as actuality the fantastic world of current magazine fiction, the movies, even television. The delight and the horror of his style is that it constantly takes off into the Never-Never Land of the mass media. After reading an advertisement, he follows with complete trust its suggestions. After reading a story or seeing a motion picture he concocts fantasies even more absurd than those which have unfolded before him. Often these are cliché-bedecked phrases or sentences: "Diamonds of the finest water gleamed at the throats of women whose beauty put the gems to shame," he claims, "and if each was not escorted by a veritable Adonis, he was at least a Greek." Again, "Not a muscle flickered in my lean jaw . . . as our little procession moved past the group of cattlemen lounging outside the Golden Girl Saloon, and their pithy comments had long since died away before I permitted myself a muttered 'Swine.' "

As in reading Benchley and Thurber, the reader sees in the assumed character here a man much like himself. In some ways, Perelman's vision of what we tend to be is the most frightening of all. His is a comic version of Huxley's *Brave New World*, or Orwell's *1984*.

He is not the only writer in this group whose comic representatives are allied with more serious fictions. Peter DeVries years ago pointed out an extraordinary resemblance between Thurber's little man and that creation of T. S. Eliot, J. Alfred Prufrock—"The same dominating sense of Predicament . . . the same immersion in weary minutiae, the same self-disparagement, the same wariness . . . the same fear, in summary, that someone . . . will 'drop a question on his plate.'" The comparison might be extended to include many characters in the modern fiction, the figure Sean O'Faolain sees as "the anti-Hero":

He is always represented as groping, puzzled, cross, mocking, frustrated, isolated in his manful or blundering attempts to establish his own personal, suprasocial codes. . . . Whether he is weak, brave, brainy or bewildered he is always out on his own. Which is why, in those fateful twenties, writers quite deliberately began . . . to dig out private caves, or air-raid shelters, of their own, and there started to compose private satires, laments, fantasies and myths in the effort to fill the vacuum left by the death of the social Hero with asocial rebels, martyrs, misfits, minor prophets, or, in short, with aberrants and anti-Heroes.

The relationship between Thurber's humor and this serious view of humanity becomes clear when one considers Thurber's personal nonhumorous statement about his own view of man:

For some curious reason Man has always assumed that he is the highest form of life in the universe. There is, of course, nothing with which to sustain this view. Man is simply the highest form of life on his own planet. His superiority rests on a thin and chancy basis: he has the trick of articulate speech and out of this, slowly and laboriously, he has developed the capacity of abstract reasoning. Abstract reasoning, in itself, has not benefited Man so much as instinct has benefited the lower animals. . . . In giving up instinct and going in for reasoning, Man has aspired higher than the attainment of natural goals; he has developed ideas and notions; he has monkeyed around with concepts. The life to which he was naturally adapted he has put behind him; in moving into the alien and complicated sphere of Thought and Imagination he has become the least well-adjusted of all the creatures of the earth, and hence the most bewildered. . . . Man . . . is surely farther away from the Answer than any other animal this side of the ladybug.

The humor of Thurber and his contemporaries is, I suggest, a comic representation of man in this grim situation. Grim, yes, if humor is taken literally, as this playful self-criticism never should be. Nurtured by a free press, native American humor has always been a purge for worries and tribulations—the struggles of a democratic nation to get going, frontier hardships, wartime tragedies, the upheavals accompanying the shift from an agrarian, rural society to an industrial, urban society. In that sense, Day, Benchley, Thurber and Perelman write in an old and honorable tradition. Also, their assumptions and beliefs are in tune with attitudes of their era. But the different nature of their assumptions and the great change in their beliefs have led them to write humor strikingly different indeed from that of the past.

7: Poetry and Language

IF THE naturalistic movement thus furnished the impetus and much of the material for a vigorous modern American literature, it still lacked adequate form and language to bring that literature to full expression as art. As Edmund Wilson pointed out in *Axel's Castle* (1931), a second movement, variously called symbolic or analytic, early provided a necessary balance and made it possible by the 1920's and 1930's for the American to put his experience of the modern world into significant works of literary art.

The book which, more than any other, represents the American writer's entrance into the twentieth century is *The Education of Henry Adams.* This modern American classic written in 1905 is the autobiography of a man who thought himself born into the eighteenth-century spirit of his grandfather and his great-grandfather (both of whom had been Presidents of the United States), and then trained in the nineteenth century for twentieth-century responsibilities. His story was like the story of the United States itself. The United States, as a nation, had been born in the eighteenth century, gained strength in the nineteenth, but in 1900 found itself on the threshold of the unfamiliar. Had the nature and process of eighteenth-century rationalism remained constant, the intervening century might have been a period of increasing intellectual confidence in the

use of reason. Had the definitions of reality and nature remained the same, one could have learned their rules and become
master of the game. What *The Education of Henry Adams*
shows is the plight of a sensitive American whose new world
was really new.

The date of a new century on the calendar brought to many
serious American writers a dramatic realization of change.
The eighteenth century had seemed a world of order. What
Henry Adams and others faced at the beginning of the twentieth century was an incredible disordering of old axioms and
definitions. This disordering had come more swiftly and more
devastatingly than even the shift from the Middle Ages into
the Renaissance. Aristotelian logic had now been displaced.
Euclidian geometry in respect to space had been overthrown.
Newtonian physics had lost its primacy. Physical reality was
constantly being redefined by geology, chemistry, biology,
physiology, physics, optics, and psychology. The older laws
of the universe no longer obtained; they were insufficient to
explain phenomena. If we speak of this situation in reference
to serious writing, we can say that literary metaphors depending on older definitions of physical reality now became invalidated. These metaphors had become invalidated because
they had come to be read not so much as metaphors but as
literal corresponding counters. Fresh metaphors demanded
fresh language taking in a new measure of reality. Fresh language, of course, conversely demanded fresh metaphors.

Twentieth-century man learned to see differently, as Cézanne
showed him. He learned to hear differently, as Schönberg did.
He learned to think differently, by means of symbolic and non-
Aristotelian logic, as Whitehead taught him. Given these
parallels, the twentieth-century writer had to learn to communicate differently if he was to represent the nature of what
was now universally regarded as true. How this change in
literary communication developed in American writing we
can see in the examples of three influential authors: Gertrude
Stein, Ezra Pound, and T. S. Eliot. Their work could not
have been written in any age but our own. Their syntax is an

expression not simply of the twentieth-century mood but of the twentieth-century mind.

Of course for Americans at the turn of the century, and afterwards, there was a sense of coming of age. There was an increasing awareness of the development of an individualized American language. American writers were no longer cultural colonials. They were free. Language freed them to be themselves, as all writers should be free, always.

Gertrude Stein expressed this feeling of linguistic liberation in a still unpublished paper which she called "American Language and Literature." What Americans did, what they could do, was not to change the English language but to make it feel different. So it could tell its own story in its own way, "using the same words as the English do," she said elsewhere, "but the words say an entirely different thing." This was the decided liberation that Gertrude Stein felt when she began to write at the end of the nineteenth century. "I found myself plunged," she said, "into a vortex of words, burning words, cleansing words, liberating words, feeling words, and the words were all ours and it was enough that we held them in our hands to play with them; whatever you can play with is yours, and this was the beginning of knowing; of all Americans knowing, that it could play and play with words and the words were all ours all ours. . . . And so," she said, "was born a new generation of writers who did not have to think about the American language; it was theirs and they had it and that was all there was to it, singing it a ragtime, Sherwood Anderson or Hemingway or Faulkner, they all had it and now what are they going to do with it, that is the question." *

What Americans were going to do with it was indeed a question. What Miss Stein was after was not just a national idiom but a contemporary idiom. Together these would emerge as a personal idiom. It is this sense of being one's self in the twentieth century that makes these American writers interesting to writers anywhere who themselves, sooner or later,

* Printed by permission of Donald C. Gallup, literary executor of Miss Stein's estate.

wanted to enter into the consciousness of the present. When Gertrude Stein strives for the achievement of a constant present in her prose she is representing by the structuring of her text what Bergson and Whitehead were asserting philosophically in regard to the now-ness of time. In following the new advances of experimental psychology as she had learned them at Radcliffe College under William James, she was exploring a new field of realism in which we know man not by description but by what he does: character is not to be conceived of in ethical terms but in individualities.

"To understand a thing," Miss Stein says, "means to be in contact with that thing and the human mind can be in contact with anything." This is a way in which to write. An early example is her short story "Melanctha," written in 1904-05 and named after the Negro girl who is its heroine. Melanctha is with Jeff, a Negro doctor who is courting her:

Jeff sat there this evening in his chair and was silent a long time, warming himself with the pleasant fire. He did not look at Melanctha who was watching. He sat there and just looked into the fire. At first his dark, open face was smiling, and he was rubbing the back of his black-brown hand over his mouth to help him in his smiling. Then he was thinking, and he frowned and rubbed his head hard, to help him in his thinking. Then he smiled again, but now his smiling was not very pleasant. His smile was now wavering on the edge of scorning. His smile changed more and more, and then he had a look as if he were deeply down, all disgusted. Now his face was darker, and he was bitter in his smiling, and he began, without looking from the fire, to talk to Melanctha, who was now very tense with her watching.

What has Miss Stein been doing? She was writing and giving a lesson in writing. First Jeff is warming, then smiling, then rubbing, then thinking, then wavering, then scorning, then bitterly talking. This is composition, is writing "truly," as Hemingway would say, "the sequence of motion and fact which made the emotion"—all this is the tenseness of Melanctha's watching. "The writer has got to get back intensity into the language," Miss Stein said.

And Melanctha loved him for it always, her Jeff Campbell now, who never did things ugly, for her, like all the men she always knew before always had been doing to her. And they loved it always, more and more, together, with this new feeling they had now, in these long summer days so warm; they always together now. . . .

Intensity of feeling (what Henry James called the amount of "felt life" contained in a work of art) has been a goal in serious twentieth-century American writing, because such achieved intensity draws the reader into the immediateness of the composition. To be immediate is not to be separated in time; it is to be closely related to whoever feels immediateness. It cuts a path toward the universal.

The search for universality, on these literary terms, is not an escape from time or geography into an air-conditioned ivory tower. The effects of the ivory-towered exile of a writer from his state and his fellow men leads to what Ezra Pound, in his *Hugh Selwyn Mauberley*, called the final literary estrangement. The artist who turns thus aside is capable of

> Nothing, in brief, but maudlin confession,
> Irresponse to human aggression,
> Amid the precipitation, down-float
> Of insubstantial manna,
> Lifting the faint susurrus
> Of his subjective hosannah.

The character of Mauberley of course is not Pound himself. Pound already, by 1915, had begun work on his immensely influential *Cantos*. By 1920 the *Cantos* had become his chief effort. Like all writers, he had primarily to do with words and their arrangement; like a twentieth-century writer he was aware that something had previously happened to language which must be rectified. "The betrayal of the word begins," he says, "with the use of words that do not fit the truth, that do not say what the author wants them to say." Pound likes to quote the answer of Confucius to the question of what Confucius would first set his mind to if made head of the government. The answer was direct: "To call people and things by their true and proper names." This is the initial problem of the artist too. "Artists are the antennae of the race," Pound states. "The one thing you should not do is to suppose that when something is wrong with the arts, it is wrong with the arts only. When a given hormone defects, it will defect throughout the whole system." "Beauty is difficult," Pound repeats in the *Cantos*.

The *Cantos* have seemed difficult to those who have been unwilling to step into the twentieth century. The *Cantos* make up a kind of epic story of the search of man for order, for what the Greeks defined as *to kalon:* order and beauty. Such a goal, or grail, of beauty is expressed through the arts, through politics, through economics, through music, through law, through literature, through all expressions of harmony made new for each age in the idiom of the age. The pilgrim hero does not exclude history from his knowledge; he is not the *naïf*. But history is not a past (that is, a concluded) event. It is a present event by the very fact that the hero now knows it in his own mind, inevitably related to everything else he now knows. Actual and vicarious experience exist simultaneously. Cue leads to conscious and unconscious response in unpredictable sequence and constant flow. The apparent incoherences of the sequence of events in Pound's *Cantos* are, in fact, a representation of the flow of the hero's consciousness. There is no abandonment of logic; there is only the substitution of a logic of the imagination. So, in Pound's scheme, like can follow like, or be contrasted with unlike; beauty can suggest beauty or disorder; one culture can be juxtaposed to another: whether classical, Renaissance, Chinese, early American Federal of Henry Adams' grandparents, or what is contemporary to ourselves. Personal symbols are side by side with traditional symbols; both are defined by what Pound calls "the voice of a nation through the mouth of one man."

Who is the man, this twentieth-century hero? In one sense he can only be the artist himself, speaking of what he knows. But the problem of the writer today, in a world of shrinking distances, is to find the hero who can stand for mankind. So the hero of Pound's *Cantos* is a true Everyman who speaks with all myths in his heart and all tongues on his lips. He is like Odysseus in Homer's *Odyssey*, and like Dante in *The Divine Comedy*, and like modern man himself in his own personal drama, as he passes through the inferno of historical experience into the *purgatorio* of reflection. Then—having learned to call things by their right names—to know the difference between good and evil, and between beauty and disorder—he is ready to reconstruct the ideal city of man which is our image of Paradise.

T. S. Eliot, in *The Waste Land*, has used a similar polyglot and ubiquitous reference, and has used the same combining logic of the imagination for his version of lost order and faded beauty. It is perhaps no accident that Eliot too should have been an American by birth, for the very nature of the American experience makes such a manner of expression seem natural. The American is not so firmly ensconced within a single inherited tradition that he is enslaved by it. So many languages and cultural strains have been brought to America by its settlers that their assimilation is comparatively easy. In facing this problem of cultural assimilation the situation of the American writer has anticipated the present situation of writers in other countries. For writers everywhere, the disruptions of two wars, the destruction of old normative values and frames of reference, and the introduction of fresh cultural impacts from other countries have brought them too into the bewildering disorder which a Henry Adams saw emerging with the twentieth century. Their goal must be a new amalgam of the local and international.

Like the American writer, and perhaps sometimes encouraged by his example, other writers have come to search for a freedom of language and syntax by which to present their own condition. It is likely that such writers will find, as these American writers have found, that traditionally imposed distinctions between prose and poetry have broken down, just as cultural boundaries have broken down. Writers of both prose and poetry now depend upon the implications of a logic of the imagination which combines public and personal symbols as an indication of the inescapable involvement of the individual. The paramount consideration of the writer, in any event, becomes words and their arrangement. To know the word properly and then to arrange it becomes, in an age which searches for order, a religious and philosophical act as well as an aesthetic achievement. So, in Eliot's *Four Quartets*, the final movement of each quartet is concerned with the theme of language. "Words strain, crack and sometimes break under the burden." And yet, as he says in the conclusion to "Little Gidding":

> What we call the beginning is often the end
> And to make an end is to make a beginning.
> The end is where we start from. And every phrase
> And sentence that is right (where every word is at home,
> Taking its place to support the others,
> The word neither diffident nor ostentatious,
> An easy commerce of the old and the new,
> The common word exact without vulgarity,
> The formal word precise but not pedantic,
> The complete consort dancing together)
> Every phrase and every sentence is an end and a beginning,
> Every poem an epitaph.

The end of an experience, any experience of an age, is where we begin our meditation upon it. It is the beginning of understanding which articulates and orders. The ordering is inevitably a new ordering, the counters used must necessarily be fresh. That is why writers like Miss Stein, and Pound, and Eliot have made even the art of writing become a subject of writing. For the art of writing involves soil and century and the freedom of an artist to be himself. And in his effort to succeed, the serious American writer has been, at least artistically, an optimist.

ARTHUR MIZENER

8: The "Lost Generation"

SOMETIME during the early 1920's Gertrude Stein, addressing one of her interminable monologues to Ernest Hemingway in her flat at 27 Rue de Fleurus, remarked that Hemingway and his contemporaries were "all a lost generation." She thus gave a name to that group of brilliant writers who appeared on the American scene during the decade following the First World War and who still dominate our fiction, as a bare list of their names will indicate. They included, among others, Hemingway himself, William Faulkner, F. Scott Fitzgerald, and John Dos Passos.

The "Lost Generation" is a somewhat misleading name for them, as perhaps a name that reflects the judgment of an age on itself always is. What this phrase describes is the generation's own feeling that there was almost nothing in the tradition they inherited, nothing in the conventional moral attitudes or political assumptions current in America in their time, that they could accept. They felt that they had to start over again from the beginning to work out a code of personal conduct they could live by and to construct a conception of the purposes of American society they could respect. "All I wanted to know," says the hero of Hemingway's *The Sun Also Rises*, "was how to live in [the world]. Maybe if you found out how to live in it you learned from that what it was all about." In this sense, then—the sense that all the maps were useless and that they had to explore a new-found land for themselves—this generation was lost.

It was, however, anything but lost in the sense that it felt despair at this situation. On the contrary, though it was fashionable in the twenties to talk about being disillusioned, these writers were filled with a typically American kind of energy and optimism. Their scorn of what seemed to them the provincialism of American manners and the narrow hypocrisy of American public life in their time is the scorn of people confident in their idealism. Sinclair Lewis' satiric attack on Main Street may be only partially successful, but not because Lewis doubted that Main Street's stupid provincialism could be defeated. What limits his success is his inability to conceive a cultivated community with which to replace Main Street. It is not despair but hope that creates the dishonest politicians, the stupid labor leaders, and the selfish businessmen who swarm through Dos Passos' *U.S.A.* They are the creations of an imagination afire with the possibilities for greatness in American life.

Nearly all the writers of the Lost Generation attacked the defects of the conventional life of their times. It is only lately, in novels like those of Louis Auchincloss or the most recent work of James Gould Cozzens, that our fiction has been able to imagine prewar America as made up of people no worse—if no better—than we ourselves are. But the best writers of the Lost Generation did something more than attack the world they grew up in; they also sought to discover what Henry James called "the great good place" that they were all sure existed somewhere in the American sensibility, and to learn how to conduct their own lives in order to live there successfully. In an important sense, all good American novels since World War I—from Fitzgerald's *This Side of Paradise* in 1920 to Cozzens' *By Loved Possessed* in 1957—are pilgrim's progresses. Fitzgerald said of the hero of his finest novel, *The Great Gatsby*, that Gatsby had "a heightened sensitivity to the promises of life," and there could hardly be a better phrase to describe the attitude of the writers of this generation. If they were lost, they were lost as explorers are, not as the damned are.

It is now possible to see how much the First World War had to do with this flowering of talent in the 1920's. America had perhaps then been a world power for some time, but it was the war that forced Americans to recognize the fact that their country was a responsible part of Western culture. The immediate—and much advertised—effect of this discovery was to make most alert Americans dissatisfied with the narrowness of American civilization, to the point where they preferred to live elsewhere. As early as 1921 Harold Stearns performed one of the symbolic acts of the decade. Having edited a symposium called *Civilization in the United States*, which concluded that there was very little, he moved to Paris. An astonishing number of the writers of the period did the same thing. But the significance of Harold Stearns's act was not his sitting throughout the decade at the Dôme in Paris; it was his editing *Civilization in the United States*. For all these writers Europe was a means to an end, something that would help them discover the possibilities in themselves as Americans.

As long as America had remained, for its own imagination, a provincial backwater, it had been difficult for most gifted Americans to take it quite seriously. The half-dozen great writers America produced in the nineteenth century were all —however reluctantly—alienated from their society, whether they went literally into exile, as Henry James did, or only metaphorically, as Hawthorne and Melville did. But the writers of the 1920's went to Europe to discover the American consciousness of experience.

The most significant thing about these writers, then, was their independently achieved but shared conviction that it was possible for an American, writing directly out of American experience, to produce major novels. When F. Scott Fitzgerald was an undergraduate at Princeton in 1916, he said to his fellow undergraduate, Edmund Wilson, "I want to be one of the greatest writers that ever lived, don't you?" If this remark was almost ludicrously brash, it was also quite serious, as the persistence of this impulse throughout Fitzgerald's career shows. He clearly believed that it was possible for him as an American to be a great writer, and this feeling had hardly existed in America before his time, in spite of—indeed, perhaps because of—the widespread ideological conviction that American democracy was a radically new and in many ways highly successful social experiment.

Young men with Fitzgerald's feeling for the possibilities of American experience suddenly appeared in all parts of the United States in the early 1920's. Fitzgerald himself was a second-generation Irish Catholic boy from St. Paul, Minnesota; John Dos Passos was the son of a successful New York lawyer whose father had been a Portuguese immigrant; Ernest Hemingway was the son of a doctor from a middle-class suburb of Chicago; William Faulkner came from a backwoods county seat in northern Mississippi, where his family had lived for over a hundred years. It made no difference. They were all convinced of the special significance of American experience, and they felt that, by discarding their parents' narrow conception of that experience, they had become free to tell the truth, the private, inner truth, about it.

Their central purpose, therefore, was to define a consciousness of experience, that heightened sensitivity to the promises of life that they were convinced was the special product of American experience. They wanted, too, to learn how to live by the dictates of this consciousness. Because they were aware that what they were trying to define was a product of American experience, they sought to realize it in the particulars of American life. As a result, their novels are preoccupied, sometimes exhaustingly preoccupied, with the minutiae of American daily life. Ever since the seventeenth century imposed on Western culture what is sometimes called the Descartian dualism, the Western world has had to live with a discontinuity between thought and nature, between the inner life of the consciousness and the outer life of the physical and social world. American society was, as it were, invented according to the theories of the seventeenth century, and one of the results is that the discontinuity between the inner life of the consciousness and the outer life of society is very marked here. The most difficult problem confronted by the novelists we are considering was that of bridging the gap between their heroes' heightened sense of the promises of life and the actualities of the society in which this heightened sensitivity was developed and had to realize itself.

Thus, for example, Dos Passos' *U.S.A.* contains three almost completely disconnected perceptions, each with its own formally isolated mode of expression. First there are the "Newsreels," montages of slogans, newspaper headlines, and snatches of popular songs. They represent the average, public awareness in the society, a sort of crude folklore. Here is a sample representing the period of the First World War:

TO THE GLORY OF FRANCE ETERNAL

Oh a German officer crossed the Rhine
   Parleyvoo

Germans Beaten at Riga . . . Grateful Parisians Cheer Marshals of France. . . .

PITEOUS PLAINT OF WIFE TELLS OF RIVAL'S WILES

Wilson's Arrival in Washington Starts Trouble

Right beside this "Newsreel" Dos Passos puts what he calls the "Camera Eye," which expresses the immediate, sensuous perception of an intensely private, turned-in sensibility, undoubtedly Dos Passos' own. Here is a sample that describes waking up in the morning:

> daylight enlarges out of the ruddy quiet, very faintly
> throbbing wanes into my sweet darkness broadens red
> through the warm blood weighting the lids warmsweetly
> then snaps on
>   enormously blue yellow pink

Between these extremes of the impersonal public sense of experience and the unique private sense of it runs the third element of the novel, the narrative of events. It is presented in a dry, neutral style that often sounds more like a sociological report than a fiction.

Though the other novelists of the period did not emphasize the discontinuities of their sensibilities, as Dos Passos does, by giving each set of feelings a separate mode of expression, these discontinuities are still apparent in their work. There is, for instance, a gap between the passages of Hemingway's *For Whom the Bell Tolls* that express his own deepest feeling for experience, like the death of Sordo, and the passages that present a history of the Spanish Civil War. Robert Jordan's death, at the climax of the novel, is a magnificent image of Hemingway's conviction that the highest form of personal virtue is "grace under pressure." But it is almost wholly unrelated to such feelings as Robert Jordan has about the values at stake in the Spanish Civil War.

Hemingway is much more successful when he isolates his characters from the social and historical circumstances that have shaped them, and then suggests those circumstances by his comments on the characters, as he does in *The Sun Also Rises*. The hero of *The Sun Also Rises* does, in fact, learn a great deal about what the world is like by slowly discovering what he calls "how to live in it," what attitudes he must take if he is to retain his self-respect. The first sentences of the book, with their brilliant and subtle suggestions about the character of American society, illustrate Hemingway's method in this book.

Robert Cohn was once middleweight boxing champion of Princeton. Do not think I am very much impressed by that as a boxing title, but it meant a lot to Cohn. He cared nothing for boxing, in fact he disliked it, but he learned it painfully and thoroughly to counteract the feeling of inferiority and shyness he had felt on being treated as a Jew at Princeton.

There is a sharp sense of American social attitudes in those three sentences, of the complex class distinctions of the great eastern universities, of the exact quality of Jewish experience in upper-class American life. There is also a clear understanding of the American concern with athletics. Who but an American would carefully disclaim being impressed by Cohn's collegiate boxing title—as if such titles were as important as those listed in *Burke's Peerage*—and at the same time suggest, by the evident irony of his disclaimer, the childish absurdity of our American preoccupation with athletics?

It is significant that Hemingway is most successful when he starts from his hero's private sense of experience and moves outward to general social judgments. This method no doubt makes it impossible for him to offer a systematic social commentary, as Dos Passos does in *U.S.A.* But it means that the social judgments he does offer are continuous with the book's central reality, the hero's personal sense of experience. In *The Great Gatsby* Fitzgerald tried to extend this method, and perhaps came close to overextending it.

To begin with, he makes his hero much more idealistic than Hemingway's about the possibilities of the personal life, so idealistic that he has no capacity for irony at all. Gatsby lives, as the narrator of the novel says, a Platonic conception of himself; he is a man who has committed himself without qualification to his vision of an ideal self; when that vision is destroyed he dies. Fitzgerald has thus maximized his hero's American idealism, his heightened sensitivity to the promises of life. It would be impossible to present such a hero directly: he would appear absurd or mad, as Hemingway's heroes—and even Hemingway himself, who sometimes imagined himself one of them —occasionally do. Fitzgerald sought to get around this difficulty by presenting his hero indirectly, through a narrator, and by having the narrator provide the irony. He does it brilliantly, but in the end we have to recognize that he means us to be wholly on the hero's side, to believe that without Gatsby's extreme idealism life is simply unlivable. When Gatsby's dream has at last been shattered, we are told, he "must have looked up at an unfamiliar sky through frightening leaves and shivered as he found what a grotesque thing a rose is and how raw the sunlight was upon the scarcely created grass. A new world, material without being real . . ."

In the second place, Fitzgerald tried to identify Gatsby's personal idealism explicitly with the social idealism that had

been the origin—and was to him still the only endurable purpose—of American society. He ends the book with the narrator
sitting on the beach back of Gatsby's deserted house, looking
out over Long Island Sound and thinking of what it had been
like there when the Dutch sailors first caught sight of it three
hundred years before.

> . . . for a transitory enchanted moment [the narrator thinks] man
> must have held his breath in the presence of this continent, com-
> pelled into an aesthetic contemplation he neither understood nor
> desired, face to face for the last time in history with something
> commensurate to his capacity for wonder.
>
> And as I sat there brooding on the old, unknown world, I thought
> of Gatsby's wonder. . . .

This is a brilliant and daring attempt to bridge the gap between the private sense of the possibilities of American life
and the public sense of what it is; but the cost is considerable.
For all *The Great Gatsby*'s brilliant surface realism, it remains
a romance, almost a fairy story in which not only the hero but
mankind become the unappreciated younger son, the male
Cinderella, whose essential fineness is destroyed by an impersonal and indifferent world.

The novels of Dos Passos, Hemingway, and Fitzgerald are
the most representative of the period. They are tragic novels
in the sense that their heroes are defeated by a society which
has not—at least not yet—fulfilled the optimistic eighteenth-
century vision of perfection to which they are all committed.
But none of these heroes ever doubts what Fitzgerald had
called his Platonic conception of himself, his idealized vision
of the personal life. Rather than compromise this ideal, they
either die—as do Gatsby and Robert Jordan—or fade from the
world—as does the hero of Fitzgerald's *Tender Is the Night*,
who quietly disappears somewhere in upstate New York, or
the hero of Hemingway's *A Farewell to Arms*, who, as the
famous last sentence of the novel puts it, "went out and left the
hospital and walked back to the hotel in the rain." For all their
practical unsuccess, these heroes are what Hemingway once
called one of his, The Undefeated. But they are also the com-

pletely isolated. Like the hero of *A Farewell to Arms*, who made a "separate peace," they have resigned from society in order to preserve the integrity of their visions of themselves.

Despite the fact that Faulkner's novels are all concerned with what he calls The Unvanquished, his heroes have not resigned from their society. Faulkner's Unvanquished is not an individual living by the dictates of his private dream of himself, as is Hemingway's Undefeated. Faulkner's Unvanquished is a community, the community of those southerners who, defeated physically in the American Civil War a hundred years ago, have refused to surrender spiritually. But Faulkner represents this community with all the romantic idealism and sense of greatness that his contemporaries bring to their individual heroes. When Faulkner is dealing with the relation between his romanticized southern community and the rest of the United States, it is easy to see how he resembles his contemporaries: in Faulkner's novels the South is always defeated but unvanquished, exactly as are the heroes of Hemingway and Fitzgerald. But when he is dealing with individuals within the southern community, he is a different kind of novelist, because these heroes—especially perhaps the Ike McCaslin of *Go Down, Moses*—work out in their own lives the dilemma of their community and are indeed almost eponymous.

These novelists, then—the Lost Generation—constitute perhaps the first coherent group of novelists in the history of American literature. They were not a school, for they only occasionally influenced each other directly, though their personal relations were, for American writers, close. Each had a distinctive voice of his own and a distinctive subject matter. But they shared a common belief in the usableness of American experience for literature that was new in America, and this common belief is all the more striking because they arrived at it spontaneously and independently. Americans have, of course, been discovering Europe and Western culture in one way or another since the days of Benjamin Franklin and Thomas Jefferson. But the Lost Generation's much advertised expatriation was a discovery of American experience as a radically different if still recognizable version of the experience of the

West as a whole, something that could be accepted without apology or self-consciousness as the material for a great act of the imagination. None of the novelists of the Lost Generation was as gifted as the great and lonely giants of nineteenth-century American fiction. But taken together, as the impulse common to their generation requires that we should take them, they constitute the finest group of novelists America has produced.

C. HUGH HOLMAN

9: The Novel in the South

OF THE novelists who stayed at home, most lived in
the South, which is more distinctively a region than is any other
section of the United States. Far more important than its
geographical boundaries—than Mason and Dixon's line and
the Mississippi River—are the boundaries of experience and
tradition which have given it a unique identity in the nation.
These experiences have taught it attitudes sharply at variance
with some of the standard American beliefs. Among these attitudes are the sense of failure, which comes from being the
only group of Americans who have known military defeat,
military occupation, and seemingly unconquerable poverty;
the sense of guilt, which comes from having been a part of
America's classic symbol of injustice, the enslavement and then
the segregation of the Negro; and the sense of frustration,
which comes from the consistent inadequacy of the means at
hand to wrestle with the problems to be faced, whether they be
poverty, racial intolerance, or the preservation of a historical
past rich in tradition.

If the characteristic American attitude is "know how," in the
South "make do" has had to be substituted for it. It is idle to
point out that each of these attitudes is the product of postures
struck willingly by the South and maintained with intractable
stubbornness. The fact remains that "Dixie" is a state of mind,

and a state of mind haunted by the imperfection, the guilt, and the tragedy of human experience as no other American's mind is. Out of such a view of experience the southern novelists in our time have fashioned a serious and often tragic literature.

In the years just after the Civil War, the southerner attempted to deny these things by the simple, but ultimately ineffectual, process of ignoring them. The southern local-color writers concentrated on the quaint, the eccentric, and the remote; and the creators of the "plantation tradition" idealized the past. Each created a synthetic South for export purposes. One was a papier-mâché world of quaint, whimsical, charming folks in mountain coves and Latin Quarters, on bayous and plantations. The other was a world over which hung, like a gossamer sheen, an idealized past crowded with happy, banjo-strumming darkies grouped about a vast mansion from between whose tall, white columns rode out "the last of the cavaliers." Both tended to convert the tragic center of southern history, the Civil War, into something as remote and glamorous as a page from Froissart.

Thus a region obsessed with the past, as no other portion of America has been, so sentimentalized that past that it became the materials of empty romance, a kind of antiseptic Disneyland, filled with idealized figures. This literary fantasy has been realized today in the guided tours, the reconstructed towns, the outdoor pageants of the tourist's South.

Against this sentimental view the first two voices that were strongly raised were those of Ellen Glasgow and James Branch Cabell, Virginians who, in their differing ways, defined the patterns which twentieth-century southern fiction was to take when it became serious and fell into the hands of that group of writers of talent who have practiced it in this century. Miss Glasgow turned upon the sentimental myth of her section the realism and irony which were her special tools. In the record of Virginia's immediate past she saw little that was comforting and nothing that was optimistic. She declared that she could not recall a time when "the pattern of society as well as the scheme of things in general, had not seemed to [her] false and even malignant." She stated that the doctrine of her best-known novel, *Barren Ground,* was that "one may learn to live, one may even learn to live gallantly, without delight."

History was, for Miss Glasgow, a tragic fable of man's lot in a hostile world, in which defeat was inevitable, but "tragedy lies, not in defeat, but in surrender." She devoted much of her career to a series of novels which collectively present a panoramic history of Virginia from the Civil War to the 1940's. Using the realistic method of Howells and Henry James, she sketched with irony and anger the social history of a doomed race of aristocrats and a democratized state wherein a sense of duty—her famed "vein of iron"—could give dignity to lives rendered unhappy by the exigencies of destiny. In the best of these novels—*The Miller of Old Church, Barren Ground,* and *Vein of Iron*—she achieved the somber tragic sense of Thomas Hardy, whom she admired greatly. In four novels laid in the city of Richmond, she employed the comedy of manners to subject Virginia assumptions to the analysis of the ironic method. Although in certain respects—command of narrative techniques and consistency of style—she fell short of the goal she set herself, Miss Glasgow saw her region in terms of its history, saw that history as a tragic fable, and imprisoned her vision in a vast and ambitiously planned group of books.

James Branch Cabell, who was nurtured on the sentimental version of Virginia history, learned early a love for the dignity, the beauty, the gallantry which it worshiped. In his maturity, however, he brought the witty cynicism of Oscar Wilde and Anatole France to bear upon a tradition which he could laugh at without ceasing to love. Where his friend Ellen Glasgow had tried to rewrite the history of her region more in accord with the facts and to give it a tragic pattern, Cabell turned from it completely and in a vastly ambitious collection of novels, *The Biography of the Life of Manuel,* explored in the history of imaginary Poictesme, between 1234 and 1750, the successive manifestations of chivalry, gallantry, and poetry. Finally he brought these qualities over the Atlantic and examined them in Virginia in such works as *The Rivet in Grandfather's Neck* and the ironic *The Cream of the Jest.* The tendency to reshape the world into something new and freshly meaningful and to represent that reshaping in a vast novelistic scheme which asserts that truth is found in men's dreams of beauty and not in their imperfect actualities is present in Cabell's work, although his basic seriousness is perhaps permanently spoiled by archness, slyness, and an uncomfortable tendency to snicker.

When a group of talented young writers in the 1920's and 1930's addressed themselves to the representation of the world through the image of their region, they followed—sometimes afar off—the paths blazed by Miss Glasgow and Cabell. These writers not only were southern but they were also the products of the same social and cultural forces that were shaping the work of other American writers. One of the most obvious characteristics of the period is that it was an age of protest against certain aspects of the American present which seemed to many to violate the American ideal. The realistic movement produced a host of social critics who busily protested against their world; they might, like Sinclair Lewis, spring from the middle-western small towns and be in passionate revolt against the "village virus"; they might, like James T. Farrell, grow up in the dingy pavements of American cities and attack the poverty of spirit which they found there. In other movements than realism the revolt against the present and past went forward, notably in Gertrude Stein's experiments with language and in the expatriates' espousal of Continental art forms. In political terms, particularly during the depth of the depression, collectivist writers like John Dos Passos attacked the capitalistic system under which they had grown up and which suddenly seemed to fail them. All these writers measured the present against the American dream and found it lacking, and they relentlessly pointed out to their fellow citizens the flaws they found.

The southern writer responded to these same impulses. The group of young poets and critics who published *The Fugitive* magazine in Nashville, Tennessee, in 1922-1925, declared that they "fled from nothing faster than the Brahmins of the Old South," and the editor of the New Orleans little magazine

The Double Dealer declared that it was time to end the treacly sentimentality of southern writing. Both were joining hands across the sea with Hemingway and Fitzgerald, with Gertrude Stein and Sherwood Anderson. But when the southern revolt against the American present was uttered, it was a call to an agrarian order. True to his traditions, the middle-western writer called for social reform and pleaded for a utopia of the future, but his southern cousin, bound by the past, looked backward for his answers. Middle-westerners went east and from Greenwich Village and New Haven chided the Middle West for its failings. Easterners went to Paris and Rome and there purified their art forms. Southerners, by and large, stayed home and sought to correct rather than to destroy their heritage.

The southern writers sought to revitalize for the modern world a view of man that the South had held since Thomas Jefferson. This view saw man as best in his relation to the soil, particularly as that relationship existed in the pre-Civil War South. This myth of a good order in the past, southern writers generally used as a weapon of attack against the bad order of modern industrialism.

They tended to seek in the past a pattern, to evolve a meaning out of large sweeps of history, converting the pattern of event into myth, and uniting the sense of tragic dignity with the irony of comedy. Some, like T. S. Stribling and Hamilton Basso, have tried to construct great connected records of social change; others, like Erskine Caldwell in his early novels, have fashioned laughter into a social weapon; still others, like Katherine Anne Porter and Eudora Welty, have used highly refined and almost poetic, brief art forms to state their visions of experience. But out of the welter of fictional accomplishment that came in the 1930's, when the southern renascence was at its height, emerge most impressively the names of Thomas Wolfe, William Faulkner, and Robert Penn Warren.

Thomas Wolfe was a man of great sensitivity and of Gargantuan appetite. He was possessed by a passionate desire to embrace all human activity, to experience all emotions, and to express through his self and the impact of the world upon that self the totality of life. Coupled with this desire to express himself was the egalitarian belief that the self whose attributes he could state was not only Thomas Wolfe but also generic man, that the world he could know and imprison on paper was America. Once he declared: "I have at last discovered my own America. . . . And I shall wreak out my vision of this life, this way, this world and this America, to the top of my bent, to the height of my ability, but with an unswerving devotion, integrity and purity of purpose."

Wolfe's "epic impulse" to define the American character and typify the American experience makes him in some respects much like Walt Whitman, but there are also notable differences. Where Whitman's self exists in an endless upward spiral of achievement—"I am the acme of things accomplished, the encloser of things to be"—Wolfe's self is trapped in the coils of time. Wolfe's characteristic feeling is not the joy of comradeship but the melancholy ache of loneliness. Man seeks everywhere, he declared, "the great forgotten language, the lost lane-end into heaven." And in this search for what he called "a stone, a leaf, an unfound door," time and the past played a strange and treacherous role, a threefold controlling function in human life, the adequate representation of which became for Wolfe the great structural problem of his novels.

The first and most obvious element of Wolfe's Time was the simple present—what he called "clock time"—the sequential flow of clock ticks, seconds, events. The second element was past time—what he called "the accumulated impact of man's experience," which makes the present and determines the moment's actions, conditioning every instance of our existence and sometimes making the unpremeditated action of an insignificant person two hundred years ago more important to our actions than the immediate sights and sounds that surround them. The third element was "time immutable, the time of rivers, mountains, oceans, and the earth; a kind of eternal and unchanging universe of time against which would be projected the transience of man's life, the bitter briefness of his day." History and memory by whose action history can be made real to the individual become for Wolfe, therefore, not casual by-products of experience as they have tended to be for many American writers, but essential elements of life.

In trying to "wreak out" this vision, Wolfe turned to many literary models—notably James Joyce, Dickens, Dostoevski, Proust, and Sinclair Lewis—and he employed the complex methods of their varying kinds of art, using physical symbols, interior monologues, objects and phrases as leitmotif, an evocation of the multiple sensory response to the physical world as directly presented as any American writer has ever achieved, and finally—apparently not trusting symbol, leitmotif, and lyric evocation to do their jobs alone—the rhetorical assertion of his meaning in dithyrambic prose poems.

In an almost pure form Wolfe represents the struggle of the novelist to record his personal experience and to find cosmic meaning in it. In short stories and short novels like *A Portrait of Bascom Hawke* and *The Web of Earth*, as well as in individual chapters or sections of his long novels, such as "The Party at Jack's" and "I Have a Thing to Tell You" in *You Can't Go Home Again*, Wolfe demonstrated that he had artistic control and the ability to realize characters and actions in compelling scenes. However, he never solved the riddle of the longer form, and his four long books—*Look Homeward, Angel, Of Time and the River, The Web and the Rock*, and *You Can't Go Home Again*—are made up of ambitious fragments giving in formless profusion a record of the novelist's own experience in his world. *Look Homeward, Angel*, an apprenticeship novel, has a form dictated by its account of growing up and is a richly evocative picture of the pains and joys of childhood and youth, but the later works lack what they most seriously need: a controlling narrative to tie their symbols together and to give them an objective reality and meaning.

In William Faulkner that controlling narrative is, at first glance, the most obvious element. For him, as it had been for Ellen Glasgow, southern history was the frame, a tragic fable of the human lot. In twenty volumes of short stories, short novels, and full-length novels, Faulkner has recorded the events of that history as he sees them impinging upon the denizens of imaginary Yoknapatawpha County in Mississippi. That county represents in its complex history and its varied citizens one of the great imaginative creations of the American mind.

As it had been for Wolfe, time is an entity in Faulkner's world. The past exists so compellingly in the present for his characters that it sometimes seems that only the past really exists for them in *Absalom, Absalom!*. Quentin Compson, trying to understand himself and his region, seeks for an answer to the riddle of the South and the self in the past events of Thomas Sutpen's life. The past and the present coexist so completely in that novel that the order in which the segments of the narrative are told defies any normal sequential sense, and Faulkner has to supply a timetable in an appendix, so that the reader can straighten out the chronology of the story. Like Wolfe, too, Faulkner often explores the inner self, particularly in *The Sound and the Fury* and *As I Lay Dying*, both of which experiment with the interior-monologue technique. But in the lonely selves of his characters are no satisfactory answers; for such answers we must see the characters against the larger context of the history of Faulkner's imaginary country. For this reason, Faulkner's work did not immediately receive the attention or the understanding that it deserves, for the large context has to be seen before the parts can be understood, and in Faulkner's case the parts came first.

That historical context is almost infinitely complex, and to simplify it to short statement is to do it the gravest violence; yet it is something like this: The South once knew an order and a tradition based on honor and personal integrity, but it was guilty of the exploitation of fellow human beings, the Indians and the Negroes. Because of this great guilt, the Civil War came like a flaming sword and ended the paradise of the noble but guilty past. After the war, noble men for ignoble reasons submitted themselves to the moral duplicity and the mechanical efficiency of the mindless new world, and the region fell into the darkness of moral decay. If it is to win its way out again, it will do it through the reawakening moral vision of its youth and the prevailing strength of its Negroes. Such a reshaping of history into myth functions in Faulkner as a controlling shape for the characters whose individual actions sometimes seem to run counter to the general pattern. It is startlingly close to a cosmic view of history, a view that seeks with passionate intensity for meanings that transcend and explain facts and particularities.

And not content with this vast frame of reference, Faulkner uses a variety of devices to assert meaning in the smaller fragments of the vast work. One of the most persistent of these has been the retelling of the Christ narrative in various forms, as an account of guilt, vicarious suffering, and attempt at expiation. In some of the early stories, written in the beginning of his career and collected as *New Orleans Sketches*, Faulkner has used the Christ story as a means of investing the actions of his books with meaning. Echoes of the Christ narrative appear in *The Sound and the Fury*, in the actions of Quentin Compson. In *Light in August*, the protagonist, Joe Christmas, believes he has a trace of Negro blood, a symbol of guilt, which he must expiate, and Faulkner bolsters this suggestion with a long chain of parallels between Joe's actions and those of the Passion Week. In *A Fable*, Faulkner moves all the way to allegory and uses the Christ story as a frame for a fable of a modern attempt to establish peace on earth.

Faulkner also employs images and symbols drawn from many sources, particularly from Freud, to strengthen and enrich his meanings, even to the extent in *The Sound and the Fury*, it has been suggested, of making the three leading male characters into personifications of the id, the ego, and the superego. Like Wolfe, too, Faulkner is not averse to rhetoric as a device for stating meaning. In fact, Faulkner's power with words is one of his most important characteristics. In recent years he has used it increasingly to state his meanings, perhaps because his creative powers are lessening, perhaps because the southern writer does not distrust rhetoric as other American writers tend to.

Faulkner also shares with Wolfe the quality of intensity. Everything in Wolfe's world is vast, every emotion is cosmic, every action gigantic. A similar intensity exists in Faulkner's world. The figures who act out the steps in their damnation on the streets and roads of Yoknapatawpha County are the creation of a nonrealistic imagination; they loom larger than life, immense in feeling and movement. Upon them sweep howling winds from the past. Their actions—even simple, homely actions—assume cosmic significance. They are lit by lurid lights and they cast vast shadows. Although they are simple, earthy, natural folks, when the furies possess them—as the furies always do in Yoknapatawpha County—they become gods and demigods. They resemble most the grim and extravagant creatures of Webster, Ford, and Marston, for they belong in the dark tragedy of the English Jacobean stage. That these figures and their actions are often redeemed by earthy humor, comic speech, and simple verisimilitude should not blind us to their essentially unearthly nature. They exist as phantasms in a cosmic dream of history, a dream that pictures the glory and the tragedy of man.

Wolfe's fury-driven and soul-searching protagonist, in his effort to state meaning, was often guilty of what seems to be empty bombast. In Faulkner through symbol, allegory, and rhetoric this fury-driven search is given objective dramatic existence. Each writer seeks not the portrayal of the world, but the discovery and enunciation of a cosmic truth.

In Robert Penn Warren's novels these tendencies and concerns are employed by a writer of great talent, great sophistication, and great intellect. The most notable characteristic of Warren's work is his serious concern with religious and philosophical ideas. He attempts to write the novel of ideas in which the essentially southern view of man is dramatized through melodramatic actions involving southern characters.

For Warren the problems of man are the twin problems of finding identity and expiating guilt. In finding identity man moves, he believes, from nontime to time, from innocence to guilt; for guilt is an inevitable property of identity. Warren repeatedly tells the story of that guilt and that search in poetry, short stories, and novels, frequently laid in the historical past or involving legendary folk characters.

Warren's novels are uniformly technical tours de force, in which the normal demands of their apparent type of fiction are set aside in order to achieve meaning through the manipulation of action and the special use of witty, knowing, and metaphysical language which can express meaning in its complexity and ambiguity. Jack Burden, the stylized and speculative narrator in *All the King's Men*, becomes the chief explicator of the universal problems which Warren finds embedded in the ambiguous career of a political demagogue, Willie Stark, and ultimately the novel is about Burden's self-discovery through Willie Stark and not about Willie Stark as a political figure.

In *World Enough and Time*, Warren deserts the formal characteristics of the historical romance to write a novel that surrenders the quality of immediacy in order to brood over the Beauchamp-Sharp murder case, an early-nineteenth-century Kentucky tragedy which had already engaged the attention of Poe, Hoffman, Simms, and others. He leaves the materials of the story essentially abstract, its characters symbolic, and Jeremiah Beaumont, who writes much of the book as a philosophic speculation, remains a symbol of man's search for the meaning of justice, death, and the end of man. In *Band of Angels*, Warren writes what looks like another historical slave narrative, loaded with melodrama, about a supposedly white girl who proves to be a Negress and is sold into slavery. Yet the story, with its extravagant action and intense emotions, is actually an exploration of the nature of freedom. In *The Cave*, through a fine-tuned use of folk voices, each carefully keyed to its place in the narrative, Warren employs the events centering around a man trapped in a cave and the attempts to rescue him to explore a number of people's search for identity, a search which is defined as seeking original innocence through escaping out of time into nontime. Each man is seeking self-recognition, of which, in *Brother to Dragons*, Warren said:

> The recognition of complicity is the beginning
> of innocence.

> The recognition of necessity is the beginning
> of freedom.

> The recognition of the direction of fulfillment
> is the death of the self.
>
> And the death of the self is the beginning of
> selfhood.
>
> All else is surrogate of hope and destitute
> of spirit.

And he once said, ". . . the story of every soul is the story of its self-definition for good or evil, salvation or damnation." Warren was not friendly to Thomas Wolfe's fiction, as is Faulkner, who considers Wolfe one of the greatest American writers. In a telling comment on Wolfe's inability to objectify his vision of experience, Warren once reminded Wolfe that Shakespeare was content to write *Hamlet*, he did not have to *be* Hamlet. Yet Wolfe's central theme, which was the soul's search for surety, the endless seeking for communion, for meaning, "the search for the father," is remarkably close to Warren's. For Warren's characters seek in the ambiguity of a world of shadows, of intermingled good and evil, to know the nature of themselves and to understand the quality of identity.

In dramatizing this tragic view of man caught in his nature and the trap of time, southern novelists have returned to a vision of human experience that is sharply at variance with that of much of America, to a vision that is essentially romantic and idealistic. The southern novelist sees man as a tragic figure rather than a mechanical victim and relates his meaning to a large structure of event and history. Wolfe, Faulkner, and Warren each has created a kind of fiction out of the materials of his region and its past which can and does counterpoise the despairing view of man that naturalism and realism have taken in our time. In expressing their revolt against the modern world they have looked backward to a tradition and an order wherein meaning is to be sought and found, man has dignity, and history is a record of a purpose. Out of these materials they have formed a fictive world of great intensity, beauty, and worth.

10: The New Criticism

MODERN AMERICAN criticism was the result of the search for a more rigorous way of defining the special qualities of a work of literary art. One of the streams which fed this movement was the reaction against romanticism—against the romantic view that the function of a work of art was to express the personality of the author and the function of the critic was to record his own emotional response to the author's achievement. This new classicism saw the literary work as distinguished by precision of imagery and by order. Those writers of the American South who deplored the chaotic individualism of modern industrial civilization and hoped for the establishment of a more traditional kind of order, both in life and in art, were reacting as southerners to the special problems of the South, and asserting the South's sense of tradition and order in the face of what they considered to be the corrupting confusions of northern industrial life. The southern agrarian movement in the 1920's was deliberately reactionary in that it wished to restore the ideals and standards of a preindustrial way of life. This mood made itself felt in literary criticism in the periodical *The Fugitive*, founded by John Crowe Ransom and Allen Tate in 1922, and edited jointly by them from 1922 to 1925.

Meanwhile, an antiromantic movement had been arising from

other sources. The English critic and philosopher T. E. Hulme had written, in the years immediately preceding his death in World War I in 1917, a series of essays in which he attacked the subjectivism and vagueness of romantic literature and advocated "dry and hard" images in poetry as well as objectivity and discipline in art in general. Hulme believed that "man is by nature bad or limited, and can consequently only accomplish anything of value by disciplines, ethical, heroic or political," and he saw one consequence of this belief as an abandonment of romantic optimism about the nature and potentialities of man. Hulme's views influenced T. S. Eliot and are reflected in Eliot's influential essay, "Tradition and the Individual Talent," which first appeared in 1917. In this essay Eliot wrote: ". . . the poet has, not a 'personality' to express, but a particular medium, which is only a medium and not a personality, in which impressions and experiences combine in peculiar and unexpected ways. Impressions and experiences which are important for the man may take no place in the poetry, and those which become important in the poetry may play quite a negligible part in the man, the personality." Eliot repudiated Wordsworth's view that poetry takes its origin in "emotion recollected in tranquillity" and asserted that "Poetry is not a turning loose of emotion, but an escape from emotion; it is not the expression of personality, but an escape from personality." Here, as in the southern critics, emphasis was on the craft, on the work of art as the significant ordering of images, rather than on the emotional effect of the work on the reader or on its autobiographical meaning for the writer. Poetry, as Eliot insisted, was to be regarded as itself and not another thing. It was not biography and it was not history, nor was it part of the history of ideas. It was a timeless pattern of meaning, to be regarded ideally as though it were contemporary and anonymous.

This last point represents a further development of Eliot's ideas by American critics of the 1930's. But it is a development of the same movement. Whether it derived from the self-consciously reactionary ideology of the Fugitives of the South, or from Hulme's insistence on precision and discipline, or from

Eliot's plea for the impersonality of art, this was a movement which had as one of its main objectives the rescuing of the work of literary art from biography and history and the discovery of its uniqueness. What is it that distinguishes the literary use of language, and in particular the poetic use of language, from other ways of using language? What is it that a poem is *uniquely?* These are the questions that the New Criticism (as it came to be called) was chiefly concerned to answer.

But it was not enough to say that poetry must be characterized by clarity and precision of imagery on the one hand and by impersonality on the other. The influence of French Symbolist poetry, which came in through Eliot as well as by other means, suggested that the image, however clear and precise as an image, should be so placed in the total pattern of imagery that it should acquire overtones of meaning far more subtle (and at the same time far more accurate) than anything that could be achieved in ordinary prose discourse. Secondly, the influence of the English metaphysical poets of the seventeenth century, which had been growing steadily since the publication of H. J. C. Grierson's great edition of the poems of John Donne in 1912, added a further criterion. This was wit. In his famous essay on the metaphysical poets in 1921, Eliot emphasized the fact that in these poets thought and feeling went together, whereas in later poets thought and feeling had become separated. "A thought to Donne was an experience; it modified his sensibility," he wrote. On the other hand, "Tennyson and Browning are poets, and they think; but they do not feel their thought as immediately as the odour of a rose." This new esteem for the English metaphysical poets meant a new esteem for intellectual toughness in poetry and for the serious use of wit. In the nineteenth century wit had, for the most part, been relegated to comic poetry. Such devices as the pun were regarded as comic and as unfit for serious poetry. But now critics demanded of poetry a tougher intellectual texture, with such witty devices as the pun used as they had been used in the seventeenth century, in order to achieve ironies and ambiguities.

With wit comes irony. In a lecture entitled "Pure and Impure Poetry," delivered at Princeton in 1943, Robert Penn Warren, a southerner by origin and well known as novelist, poet, and critic, summed up a generation of discussion about the importance of irony in poetry. He insisted that in, say, a love poem the poet must not be naïvely solemn about the purity and intensity of his feelings; he must, if his poem is to be insured against ridicule and parody, include also some kind of ironic counterstatement. Love is pure and beautiful and passionate; but it is also lusty and physical and comic. If the poet does not show any awareness at all of the latter aspects, he makes himself very vulnerable to mockery. Warren contrasts the gardens of Victorian love poets with the garden in Shakespeare's Verona where Romeo and Juliet exchanged their passionate avowals while outside Mercutio made his bawdy jokes. "On what terms does a poet make his peace with Mercutio?" Warren asks. There are many ways, he replies. The important thing is that the poet must make his peace with Mercutio—must, that is, somehow include an ironical counterstatement to his principal emotional statement. The poet must not be the naïve hero of his own poems. That is what Shelley was, in the eyes of the New Criticism, and that is why Shelley was a less good poet than Donne or than Pope or than Gerard Manley Hopkins, for these latter poets all use wit and irony in one way or another to modify or comment on their surface meaning.

The modern movement has been very much aware of the ways in which the rhetoric of mass communication has vulgarized meaning. That is why, Allen Tate argued in an essay entitled "Tension in Poetry" in 1938, "many poets are driven to inventing private languages, or very narrow ones." It is "because public speech has become heavily tainted with mass feeling." The literary interest of a poem, Tate argued in this essay, does not lie in its simple communication of a line of meaning moving toward a conclusion which is the "point" of it all; nor does it lie simply in its simple embodiment of the poet's autobiographical emotion. The *extension* of the poem, its logical movement from one point to the next and so to its conclusion, and its *in*tension, the poet's emotional charge and figurative development, are both less significant than what he calls the *tension*, "the full organized body of all the extension and intension that we can find in it." The full complexity of poetic meaning transcends both the paraphrasable movement of thought and the metaphorical development at any point. Poetry, he insists, is not mere communication of ideas or attitudes; it is a complex patterning of meaning to be read and appreciated *as* a complex patterning of meaning.

A similar argument is found in John Crowe Ransom's essay, "Poetry: A Note in Ontology," written in 1934. Ransom divides poetry into three kinds. There is "physical poetry" which tries to capture the precise qualities of things by using the kind of hard, clear, accurate images advocated by T. E. Hulme and by the Imagist poets, who, in some degree, stemmed from Hulme. But the accurate presentation of human reactions to physical objects, though a worthy activity, is not really satisfactory: it is too limited. Ransom's second kind of poetry is what he calls "Platonic poetry," which is poetry that seeks to move the reader to take up a particular ethical attitude. He considers this "bogus poetry," not really poetry at all, and charges Shelley and Tennyson, among other nineteenth-century poets, with having produced it. His third kind is "metaphysical poetry," which is poetry that uses metaphorical and other kinds of figurative language to shock the reader into new and exciting perceptions of its subject.

Elsewhere, Ransom has drawn an important and influential distinction between the *texture* and the *structure* of a poem. The texture is the quality of the expression at any given point, enriched by every kind of appropriate metaphorical device so as to embody the full quality of the things being referred to; the structure is the paraphrasable argument. Scientific discourse for Ransom is all structure and no texture: it deals in generalities, not in particularities. Poetry has both structure *and* texture, and it is only by running the poem through the intricacies and particularities of the local texture as it proceeds that the structure is made truly meaningful and truly poetic. The similarity of this view to Tate's theory of "tension" is part of a family resemblance between all those modern critics who are concerned to separate out the special differentiating qualities of poetic as distinct from scientific or historical discourse. Although most of these critics are concerned with literary art in general, they nearly always prefer to illustrate their points with reference to lyrical poems.

Meanwhile, I. A. Richards in England had been developing views about the nature of poetic meaning and its distinction from scientific meaning which were to have considerable influence on the whole modern critical movement. Poetry, Richards argued in his book *Science and Poetry* in 1926, does not deal with scientific or historical fact. It deals with what he calls "pseudo-statements," and "a pseudo-statement is true if it suits and serves some attitude or links together attitudes which on other grounds are desirable." Richards distinguished between what he called "referential meaning," which belonged to science and other kinds of informative writing, and "emotive meaning," which belonged to poetry and had for its function not the communication of facts or ideas but the communication of a valuable state of consciousness. Few later critics have accepted this particular aspect of Richards' thought—which is expounded in his *Principles of Literary Criticism*, 1924—but the investigation of the ways in which language works, which Richards' views led him to, has been extremely influential.

In his endeavor to illustrate and expound his view of "emotive meaning," Richards developed a much closer and more sensitive reading of literary texts than had hitherto been common among critics. He brought the study of semantics, of what he called "the meaning of meaning," into literary criticism, and in doing so helped to encourage the careful analytic treatment of individual poems that has been so characteristic of modern criticism. We have already seen how the southern critics, encouraged by the tradition of criticism that stemmed from T. E. Hulme and T. S. Eliot, had insisted on exploring the literary artist's craftsmanship in meticulous detail and had thus both practiced and encouraged a rigorous analytic criticism. With the influence of Richards there came a further impetus to the same kind of analytic rigor. It is hardly sur-

prising, therefore, that the New Criticism has been characterized by subtle analytic procedures and that the more relaxed
and personal critical discourse of much nineteenth- and early
twentieth-century criticism, with its large use of generalizations, should have been strongly attacked by the most representative American criticism of our time.

Studying the writer's craft: that is how one could describe
much of the New Criticism. What goes on in a work of
literary art—especially in a poem? How does language work
in it? How is imagery used? What totality of meaning is
achieved and in what way? These are the questions the New
Criticism asks, and asks always with the underlying intention of
showing how the work of literary art is "itself and not another
thing," never to be confused with ordinary kinds of descriptive,
informative, or persuasive writing. One of the most acute and
versatile of the New Critics, who studies the writer's craft with
a peculiarly appealing kind of wit and even gaiety, is R. P.
Blackmur. Blackmur's many collections of critical essays investigate the ways in which ideas can be absorbed by craft into
poetic meaning and the relationship between ideas, imagination,
and craftsmanship.

In its effect on the academic study of English, the New
Criticism has helped to discredit the survey course, with its
large historical generalizations and its treatment of literature as
documents in the history of ideas, and focus on the detailed
analytic description of particular works. Textbooks intended to
train the student in analytic description have been pouring off
the presses over the last twenty years. Notable among these
is *Understanding Poetry*, by Robert Penn Warren and Cleanth
Brooks, first published in 1938. Cleanth Brooks has been an
important practitioner of the New Criticism and a main
propagandist for it. In his book, *Modern Poetry and the
Tradition*, published in 1939, he approached English poetry
from the point of view of one who adopted the criteria of
symbolic use of imagery, complexity of organization, irony,
and paradox—criteria which owed much to the critical ideas
of Hulme, Eliot, the Fugitive group, I. A. Richards, and the
English critic F. R. Leavis. As a result, he exalted every poet

in the "symbolist-metaphysical" tradition and depressed those who were not. In later critical studies Brooks, like other New Critics, has shown greater catholicity of appreciation, but even so he will admire no poet whom he cannot prove to be ironical and paradoxical. In an essay entitled "The Language of Paradox," which appeared in 1942 and has been reprinted in several anthologies of criticism, Brooks maintained that "there is a sense in which paradox is the language appropriate and inevitable to poetry. It is the scientist whose language requires a language purged of every trace of paradox; apparently the truth which the poet utters can be approached only in terms of paradox." He went on to show that even in a poem which may seem perfectly simple and straightforward on the surface, such as Wordsworth's sonnet on Westminster Bridge, there is an expression of a paradoxical situation, and that it is out of this paradoxical situation that the power of the poem arises.

The scientist employs referential meaning, argued Richards, while the poet employs emotive meaning. For John Crowe Ransom, scientific discourse uses structure but not texture, while poetic discourse uses both. For Brooks, the scientist needs a language purged of paradox while the poet needs paradox. One can see here the common interest in differentiating between science and poetry that has been such an important feature of modern critical theory and practice. In a scientific age—the unspoken assumption seems to be—poetry cannot compete with science on any common ground; poetry (and imaginative literature in general) must be shown to be something absolutely separate, both in its way of handling language and in its value, if it is to be properly defended.

One result of this insistence on the uniqueness of the literary, and especially the poetic, way of using language has been a certain amount of friction between the literary historian and the literary critic. The critic is concerned with the structure of meaning in a given work of literary art, while the historian seeks to make generalizations about the works of a period and their relation to the culture which produced them. The historian cannot help seeing works of literature as in some sense documents in the history of ideas; he is also very much aware of the shifting meanings of words and the degree to which the meaning of works written in the past cannot be fully appreciated without some knowledge of the intellectual habits of the period. The New Critics' tendency to see a poem as a timeless structure of meanings which can be analyzed without reference to the specific meanings of words at a specific moment in time has ruffled some of the conservative literary scholars who thought that the New Criticism was claiming complete freedom from historical discipline. It is clear by now, however, that the New Critics never intended to claim such freedom; they would regard, rather, any historical investigation of what certain words meant at a certain time, or of a relevant pattern of ideas which belonged to the period when the work was produced, as a necessary preliminary establishment of the text (like the editing of a manuscript, or perhaps like learning a foreign language before one can read anything written in that language). Such activity they would consider as often necessary, but *precritical*. Criticism for them begins with an investigation of the way words are made to work in the given example of literary art.

Another result of the analytic method of the New Critics, and a more serious charge against it, is that it has reduced all poetry to a formula (such as paradox, or "structure and texture") and that it puts a premium on mere ingenuity of analysis. Anything can be proved to be paradoxical or ironical if the critic tries hard enough, and who is to determine at what point the critic ceases to read what is really present in the text and begins to read into the work fantastic ingenuities of meaning that are not in any real sense *there?* The English critic William Empson, who began as a pupil of Richards and who has produced some brilliantly ingenious analyses of meaning in literary works, has had considerable influence on the younger American New Critics. But American scholars have challenged Empson's interpretations on historical grounds and in terms of the conventions within which the particular authors wrote. The words *could not* have had the meanings he attributes to them and an analysis that assumes that they have these meanings takes us away from rather than more deeply into the work in itself.

It has been argued that the New Criticism has encouraged the exercise of analytic ingenuity by people who have no real awareness of what literature is, that it has encouraged the use of pretentious jargon and removed criticism into a highly special-ized technical area where it cannot be read or appreciated by the ordinary reader, so that it is read only by other critics. It has further been argued—and this perhaps is the gravest of the charges that has been brought against the New Criticism —that it has ignored altogether the relation of literature to life, the ways in which literature illuminates life and the insights and satisfactions it really gives to readers, and has reduced it to an elaborate puzzle game of interest only to experts. In their protest against vulgar misconceptions, against confusions be-tween the poetic and the scientific uses of language, against confusions between poetry and rhetoric or between works of literature and works of direct moral edification, the New Critics, it has sometimes been argued, may have gone too far and landed themselves in the position where they seem to be implying that the ultimate aim of art is to produce the critic's analysis of it, and that the function of criticism is to train other critics to train other critics to train other critics in a barren academic succession of ingenious analyzers who talk only to each other.

Every critical movement can be taken to ridiculous extremes, and the New Criticism has had its narrow and extreme practi-tioners. Further, no critical position can ever hope to tell the whole truth about either the nature of art in general or the quality and meaning of a particular work. But fruitful critical movements draw attention to forgotten or hitherto unrealized aspects of art. The modern reaction against a faded romanti-cism was a necessary one; the insistence on strictness of analysis, on "close reading" of texts, was a salutary corrective to the chatty generalizations which often passed for criticism at the beginning of this century. The New Criticism, with its cry of "Look at the work! Examine the text!" taught readers to approach works of literature directly rather than through pre-digested "appreciations" or potted histories which told them beforehand, in the most generalized terms, what qualities to find. If the days are now over when students could pass an examination in a literature course simply by memorizing lists of adjectives applicable to particular writers, this is in large meas-ure an achievement of the New Criticism. While it may *not* be true that all good poetry is paradox, or that the counter-pointing of structure and texture is always what goes on in a poem, it *is* true that to understand and appreciate a work of literature properly you must *read* it. The New Criticism has taught a whole generation to read. If it sometimes taught it to read out of the human context which alone gave meaning to what was written, the fault was perhaps inevitable in a move-ment which sprang in large measure in reaction against romantic gush.

The term "New Criticism," as it has for some time been generally used, is often restricted to mean that type of rigorous analytic description of particular literary works, with its close reading of the text, which developed out of the modern Neoclassical reaction. There are, however, other significant phases of modern American criticism which are also part of the New Criticism in its larger definition. Interest in the way in which language works in poetry led to a study of metaphor and its place in poetic expression, and the study of metaphor was by some critics linked with the study of myth. The study of myth, in turn, was encouraged by new developments in anthropology and psychology. Studies of the place of myth and symbol in primitive civilizations and in early literature were linked to semantic and critical studies of the way language works in poetry. The German-born professor Ernst Cassirer, in his *Philosophy of Symbolic Forms*, published between 1923 and 1929, provided a philosophical basis (largely Kantian) for this new study of myth and symbol, and Suzanne K. Langer developed Cassirer's theories in *Philosophy in a New Key*, published in 1942, an influential book which explored myth as a way of knowing; Mrs. Langer's later book, *Feeling and Form*, published in 1953, applied this analysis to the presentation of a symbolist view of the arts. Thus anthropological, psychological, semantic, and critical ideas came together to encourage what has been called the "myth and metaphor" aspect of the New Criticism. The study of folklore and of ritual was also called on to illuminate the ways in which poetic language works and to explain the significance of certain basic plots in drama and fiction.

The psychology drawn on by the "myth and metaphor" school was more often that of Carl Jung than that of Freud. Jung's concept of racial memory and the collective unconscious, and his notion of "archetypes"—images which derive their power from their long history in the collective unconscious—proved to be especially fruitful for literary criticism. In England, Maud Bodkin's book, *Archetypal Patterns of Poetry*, published in 1934, investigated some of the ways in which these primordial images and situations accounted for the impact made by certain great works of literary art. Since then, many American critics have developed this kind of analysis much further. Richard Chase, in *The Quest for Myth*, published in 1949, goes so far as to see all genuine poetry as a form of myth. This kind of approach is particularly helpful when dealing with such obviously symbolic and myth-using writers as Herman Melville and Nathaniel Hawthorne; it has been used effectively, too, in discussing Shakespeare, especially such a play as *King Lear*, which has powerful mythic elements. The danger of the method is that it can be simply *reductive*, reducing great and complex works of art to the equivalent of primitive myths, and making *King Lear* the equivalent of a folk tale or a nursery rhyme. The value of the method, on the other hand, lies in pointing up the basic kinds of human interest and meaning that can be found in literary works and in emphasizing the continued relevance of literature to themes fundamental in all human experience. In this respect it acts as a counterbalance to the more formalist techniques of those New Critics who are most concerned with demonstrating ambiguities and complex patterns of meaning. A symposium on *Myth*, published by the American Folklore Society in 1955, summed up much of the work done by recent criticism in relating the anthropological and psychological study of myth to the criticism of literature.

It would be a mistake to give the impression, in discussing the development of New Critical techniques of analysis and close reading or the use of myth in investigating poetic metaphor and dramatic plots, that the critics work together in schools, each school sticking rigidly to its own method. Some critics, of course, *are* rigid in their attitude and their method, but in others we find different methods being used together or a particular method being used in a special and personal way. Ransom has quarreled with Richards' view of the necessity of irony in poetry and with Eliot's notion of how the poet operates; Tate and Ransom both disagree with Richards' analysis of poetic meaning; and there are many other differences between the New Critics. Each has his individual voice—the almost quizzical courtliness of expression in Ransom; Blackmur's delight in exploring the tricks of the writer's trade; Tate's combination of acidity and fervor; Cleanth Brooks's pedagogical persuasiveness; Robert Penn Warren's sly use of analogy.

There are other individual voices among the New Critics. Kenneth Burke's complex discussions of the relation between psychology, rhetoric, and literary form represents an original development of a number of modern tendencies. Yvor Winters' attack on Eliot's poetry and criticism and his insistence on the rational structure of a poem shows a different kind of modern classicism from the one I have discussed. The broadly based combination of social and psychological investigation to be found in the criticism of Edmund Wilson yields something much less technical and of more appeal to the general reader than the characteristic product of the New Criticism. Lionel Trilling is another influential critic who has benefited by the analytic disciplines developed by the New Critics while cultivating a kind of criticism which relates works of literary art in a large Humanist way to general cultural interests; Trilling has also learned a great deal from modern psychology.

Some of the most interesting modern criticism has developed in conjunction with parallel movements in creative literature.

Many of the New Critics are also poets or novelists. Robert Penn Warren and Allen Tate are both; Ransom is a poet; so is Yvor Winters. So while modern criticism has become much more specialized and technical than it has ever been before in the English-speaking world, it has nevertheless been working in close association with creation. T. S. Eliot's critical essays reflect the poetic ideals he was implementing in his poetry; John Crowe Ransom's quietly witty and beautifully shaped poems show that combination of imagistic precision and metaphorical subtlety that he advocates in his criticism. Richard Blackmur, too, has written poems which show him putting into practice some of the theories of craftsmanship which he discusses in his critical essays. It has been argued, and with some justice, that a critic who is also a creative writer will be inclined to defend in his criticism only the kind of creation that is congenial to his own creative talent. Thus the exaltation of the symbolist-metaphysical tradition in poetry above other traditions can be attributed to the fact that the poet-critics who have brought about the revival and high esteem of this tradition were all temperamentally inclined to use it in their own poetry.

The spirit of the age and the psychological and emotional needs of the first half of the present century helped to bring about this preference. The playing down of the romantics and the playing up of metaphysicals and symbolists—the playing down of Shelley and Tennyson and the playing up of Donne and Hopkins, and in American poetry the preference of Emily Dickinson to Walt Whitman—was bound up with the deepest feelings of the age. Ideally, it can be maintained that the true critic should stand above changes in literary fashion and appreciate the best produced by different traditions. But when the critic is as closely associated with the creative movement of his day as the modern critic has been, he will inevitably become a defender and expounder of it. Thus Wordsworth, in his preface to the second edition of the *Lyrical Ballads*, produced a theory of poetry which justified his own practice. Eliot and Tate and Ransom have done the same. Wordsworth needed to undervalue eighteenth-century English poetry if he was to free himself to operate in the way that suited his genius.

Perhaps the antiromanticism of the New Criticism represented a similar creative need.

At any rate, it can be confidently claimed that the twentieth century in America has proved to be the greatest period of criticism known in either British or American literary history. The most creative minds turned to criticism—indeed, Richard Blackmur has argued, with pardonable exaggeration, that the most creative aspect of modern American literature *is* its criticism. Of course, the numerous routine practitioners of fashionable critical techniques are anything but creative, but it is unfair to judge a movement by its routine practitioners. At its best, the new criticism explores the nature of literary meaning with new kinds of awareness and probes with delicate and subtle curiosity into questions which earlier critics felt were mysteries to be dealt with only in terms of exclamations of wonder. It is perhaps wrong of a critic to believe that everything about creative literature can be explained by descriptive analysis, but between the two extremes of determination to investigate what goes on in a work of art and the cultivation of incoherent wonder, the modern mind will certainly choose the former.

So we come back to the term "classical" again. It is classical to believe that the inquiring mind can explain all, and romantic to believe on the other hand that the central truths about art are mysteries which can only be apprehended intuitively. The New Criticism is with the inquiring mind all the way. The nature of its inquiry has been in part determined by its insistence on differentiating literary art from other kinds of writing, so that it tends to discuss not *all* the qualities of literary art but only its differentiating qualities. Thus Cleanth Brooks, as we have seen, maintains that all poetry is paradox and does not sufficiently inquire whether it must not be something else as well in order to be poetry. What imaginative literature has in common with other kinds of discourse is not, as a rule, discussed by the New Critics.

The credit balance of the New Criticism remains immensely impressive. I have said that it taught a generation to *read*. I should add that it taught it also to reflect on *meaning*, to pay attention to what a work of literary art really means. If it does not directly illuminate the ways in which art explores the meaning of experience, it often does so indirectly by increasing our awareness of how language functions in literature. Language was created by men in response to human needs, so that in the last analysis the more profoundly we appreciate how language works the more we understand about men. The New Critics, with their insistence on studying the craft, shied away from any emphasis on this implication. But it is there none the less. They tell us what literature is, how it works, and we are left to infer why it is important. That is a sufficiently remarkable achievement.

STEPHEN E. WHICHER

11: The Art of Poetry

THE "difficult intellectual" poem in America during the years of the long armistice was actually, of course, anti-intellectual, like modernist poetry in America and Europe. It made a direct assault on the modern dissociation of "feeling" and "thought," to which Eliot had called attention, and experimented in ways and means to achieve the image—in Pound's sense, "that which presents an intellectual and emotional complex in an instant of time."

The work of such poets was part of the great effort to renew the language of the tribe which had guided European verse since Yeats and the French Symbolists, and which began much earlier in America with Whitman and Poe. Such work demands not so much thought as attention. "Every great and original writer," Wordsworth said, "must create the taste by which he is to be relished." For many modern American poets this necessity has seemed inescapable for every serious writer, whether great or not: each must create not just poems but a language. The difficulty of their work, then, is no more and no less than the difficulty of any new speech. In this chapter I shall try to say something to reduce this difficulty by an examination of three typical poets of this kind: E. E. Cummings, William Carlos Williams, and Wallace Stevens.

We begin with the "bad boy" of modern American poetry,

Edward Estlin Cummings. His literary productions, from the first incredulous glimpse of the typography to the last indignant discovery of his meaning, are nicely calculated to shock conventional minds. His life has fitted his work. Son of a Harvard teacher and Boston minister, he spent three months in a French detention camp during World War I, under suspicion of sedition, an experience treated in his first and best book of prose, *The Enormous Room*, and after the war he lived a Bohemian life in Paris and New York while he gradually established a reputation as an avant-garde poet, playwright, and painter. His successive volumes bear such titles as *&*, *Is 5*, *W*, *1 x 1*, *EIMI* (I am), *XAIPE* (Hail), and one book has no title at all. Clearly here is a poet who has dedicated himself to Conspicuous Difference.

Those who will trouble to look twice at his nonsense will find a shrewd intelligence behind it. The typographical madness, for example, has method in it. Cummings uses typography in many poems like the interpretative marks in a musical score, to suggest how he wants them read: spaces indicate pauses, the absence of them continuity, parentheses and the lack of other punctuation enhance a delicate, suspended effect, capital letters are touches of emphasis, etc. The purpose in all this is the perfectly serious and legitimate one of forcing us to read his poems as poetic performances rather than as prose statements. The same is true of his wrenching of sense and grammar. When Cummings writes, for instance, "Anyone lived in a pretty how town," he is nudging us to take a second look at such well-worn words: How would a town look of which we exclaim "How pretty!"? So when he calls the human race "manunkind" he is inviting us to ask whether the name for our species does in fact still fit what we have become. Cummings has exhausted his very considerable ingenuity to get us to pay attention to the primary elements of poetry, sound and words. His poems are five-finger exercises in the art of reading verse.

They are skillfully constructed, for all their arbitrary appearance on the page. In the one I am about to quote, note the internal echoes—there are an amazing number of them; notice

the repetition of key words, like "carefully"; and note the
way the poet varies his phrases when he repeats them, like a
skillful musician. Yet the whole remains a distillation of the
simple speech that is appropriate to the sophisticated innocence of this poem. A typical trick is the placing of "perhaps"
in the first line. It is used as an adjective—or perhaps we should
understand the first line to mean, "Spring perhaps is like a
hand." In any case, the unusual word order underlines the
tentative, exploratory tone of this piece of mood painting and
is not untrue to the possible order of casual speech.

> Spring is like a perhaps hand
> (which comes carefully
> out of Nowhere)arranging
> a window, into which people look(while
> people stare
> arranging and changing placing
> carefully there a strange
> thing and a known thing here)and
>
> changing everything carefully
>
> spring is like a perhaps
> Hand in a window
> (carefully to
> and fro moving New and
> Old things,while
> people stare carefully
> moving a perhaps
> fraction of flower here placing
> an inch of air there)and
>
> without breaking anything.

Cummings' poems, like this one, are often deliberately simple
His specialty is the renewal of the cliché. He will take a stock
poetic subject like spring, young love, or childhood, and by
verbal ingenuity, without the irony with which another
modern poet would treat such a topic, create a sophisticated
modern facsimile of the "naïve" lyricism of Campion or Blake.
His forms are also often "stock"; clear away the typographic
camouflage and one may reveal a sonnet or other traditional

lyric form. Superficially the most shocking of moderns, Cummings is actually one of the least radical. For this reason also he is a good modern to begin on. Led by what is familiar in him to tolerate what is novel, one is better prepared for the "deep" innovations of Eliot or Stevens.

In posture and subject matter Cummings might be dubbed "the last of the romantic egoists." His world is divided into two parts: "I" (and "you") and "mostpeople." "Life, for mostpeople," writes Cummings, "simply isn't. . . . What do mostpeople mean by 'living'? They don't mean living. They mean the latest and closest plural approximation to singular prenatal passivity which science, in its finite but unbounded wisdom, has succeeded in selling their wives. . . . You and I are human beings; for whom birth is a supremely welcome mystery, the mystery of growing: the mystery which happens only and whenever we are faithful to ourselves. . . . Life, for eternal us, is now; and now is much too busy being a little more than everything to seem anything, catastrophic included."

This is clearly a highly dramatized simplification of the romantic division between the self and the "loveless, everanxious crowd." Whereas in an original romantic like Walt Whitman, the "myself" reaches out to include the world, here it withdraws to exclude it. Cummings' "I" is a sort of enchanted garden apart from the crowd where the self can wall out what it dislikes and hug its uniqueness. His poems thus fall into two parts, "innocent" hymns to the life of the self and rough satires on "mostpeople." With the passage of time the satire has become steadily more nihilistic as Cummings has repeated his comprehensive rejection. On the other hand, the affirmative lyrics have become steadily stronger, as Cummings has moved from a fragile poetics full of vague "flowers" and "petals" to a set of well-ordered techniques for eclipsing the prosaic denotations of words and weaving his poem of the coronas of significance that are left. Cummings' content is fixed and narrow and, if one likes, sentimental. His "semantic wit," however, has no match among modern poets. And among so many modern prophets of doom, it is good to have one such jaunty and affirmative figure, even when one soon realizes that the exclusiveness of his Yes and the inclusiveness of his No leave little but mood to choose between him and them, after all.

Our second example is William Carlos Williams, who also, as a modern poet must, has stubbornly gone his own way and created a kind of poetry which follows no rules but its own. Perhaps one reason for Williams' strength is the discipline of his profession, since he has combined a career as a poet with a busy professional life as a doctor in Paterson, New Jersey, often working with the poorest kind of patients and seeing the biological facts of life, as a doctor must, without a protecting veil of sentiment and illusion. The resulting toughness, without making him callous, has sinewed his verse.

His ruling objective has been to build a poetry of American speech. He regards this aim, correctly enough, as a continuation of the revolt against tradition initiated by Whitman and is probably Whitman's greatest admirer among contemporary poets. Like Whitman, he insists vigorously on the special task of the American poet, to the point of sounding a bit old-fashioned in a time when the American poet has left behind the adolescent need to stress his difference. Where Carl Sandburg, sharing such convictions, has adopted something like Whitman's manner, Williams has rejected Whitman's practice for one built on the "free verse" of the Imagist school that flourished briefly under Pound's leadership. He also seeks "direct treatment of the 'thing'" and the rhythm "of the musical phrase, not the metronome." He has become, among other things, a kind of modern Robert Herrick in that, like the Imagists, he is willing to trust the exactness of his notation of some small fact to raise it without comment to poetic significance. His main concern, however, has been to render the peculiar music inherent in American speech habits and to develop without regard to the traditions of a foreign literature the forms proper to that music. Often the line divisions of his poems are little more than a device to force the reader to move through an apparently prosaic statement slowly enough to notice each of its rhythmic elements and savor its unique cadence. Like Robert Frost, he is willing to jettison the "poetic" in order to get us to hear the poetry inherent in the actual.

Like Frost also, he risks and sometimes deserves the verdict, "This is not poetry." He is, nevertheless, a major poet because, on the one hand, he often expertly discharges the obligation to lift speech into music, and, on the other, because his poems do more than capture fact, whether speech or image; they catch the glancing movements of the creating mind itself, are *psychological* notations worked up into artistic wholes, and thus hold the mirror up to a sensibility which turns out to be an unusually interesting one. I say "sensibility" because Williams is not interesting as a thinker; he is as unintellectual as Whitman, and the thought in his verse, like the thought in O'Neill's plays, only exposes the author. But the vigor and subtlety with which the sensibility that controls these poems leaps from image to image, voice to voice, according to a strong subjective logic deep below the surface gives them the kind of depth and power which only a superior poet can command. The best illustration of this power is in the early books of Williams' long poem, *Paterson*, where, in the manner of Pound's *Cantos*, by a musical interweaving of themes and images, he attempts with sometimes impressive success to create an order from the thundering chaos of his contemporary America.

The following lyric illustrates some of these qualities. Beginning as an admiring description of racing boats, or yachts, it moves suddenly as the race starts into a surrealistic vision of the "horror of the race." The eye, if not the ear, can notice how touches of rhyme and alliteration subtly accent the expert rhythmic pattern. The title is part of the poem:

The Yachts

contend in a sea which the land partly encloses
shielding them from the too heavy blows
of an ungoverned ocean which when it chooses

tortures the biggest hulls, the best man knows
to pit against its beatings, and sinks them pitilessly.
Mothlike in mists, scintillant in the minute

brilliance of cloudless days, with broad bellying sails
they glide to the wind tossing green water
from their sharp prows while over them the crew crawls

ant like, solicitously grooming them, releasing,
making fast as they turn, lean far over and having
caught the wind again, side by side, head for the mark.

In a well guarded arena of open water surrounded by
lesser and greater craft which, sycophant, lumbering
and flittering follow them, they appear youthful, rare

as the light of a happy eye, live with the grace
of all that in the mind is feckless, free and
naturally to be desired. Now the sea which holds them

is moody, lapping their glossy sides, as if feeling
for some slightest flaw but fails completely.
Today no race. Then the wind comes again. The yachts

move, jockeying for a start, the signal is set and they
are off. Now the waves strike at them but they are too
well made, they slip through, though they take in canvas.

Arms with hands grasping seek to clutch at the prows.
Bodies thrown recklessly in the way are cut aside.
It is a sea of faces about them in agony, in despair

until the horror of the race dawns staggering the mind,
the whole sea become an entanglement of watery bodies
lost to the world bearing what they cannot hold. Broken,

beaten, desolate, reaching from the dead to be taken up
they cry out, failing, failing! their cries rising
in waves still as the skillful yachts pass over.

Our last and perhaps greatest example of the modern "difficult" poets is Wallace Stevens. He also, like Dr. Williams, gave
no comfort to those who would weep for the plight of the
artist in the modern world, since he reconciled with no apparent conflict or regret a steady, sober career as lawyer in
New York and insurance executive in Hartford, Connecticut,
with the production of poems which his business associates, if
they ever looked at them, surely would regard as not sober at
all. Poetry excepted, there was nothing of the bohemian about
Stevens. "It gives a man character as a poet to have a daily
contact with a job," he said. "I doubt whether I've lost a
thing by leading an exceedingly regular and disciplined life."

Everything Stevens did impresses one as disciplined and deliberate, and the startling eccentricities of his first and best book, *Harmonium*, are no exception. A glance down the table of contents is enough to warn us that we are dealing with a man who intends to be different: "The Comedian as the Letter C"; "The Worms at Heaven's Gate"; "Floral Decorations for Bananas"; "The Emperor of Ice-Cream"; "Thirteen Ways of Looking at a Blackbird"; etc. The content of these poems is often as *outré* as the titles. Yet he can be read, and, with a few basic clues and the attention all new art works have a right to ask, his poems can reveal themselves as among the most serious and beautiful of modern verse.

The first thing to recognize is that Stevens is a "poet's poet"; that is, he is as much interested in how he writes as in what he has to say, or more. R. P. Blackmur defines him, in the words of Logan Pearsall Smith, as one of "these artists who derive their inspiration more from the formal than the emotional aspects of their art, and who are more interested in the masterly control of their material, than in the expression of their own feelings, or the prophetic aspects of their calling." The open preference in modern abstract painting for a formal rather than a presentational art has had a strong influence on Stevens' verse. Thus, the details of Stevens' poetic world, his images and vocabulary, are often precious and exotic, obviously "poetic," as if he wished to insist on the difference between art and life.

In the following poem, for example, we have a pattern of words "abstracted" from the subject as a cubist painting is abstracted from the geometrical shapes of a real-life scene. The pattern in this case is mobile; the basic motion is circular. The poem is still a presentation of an emotion, not "pure" poetry, but the main interest is aesthetic. Even the title calls attention to the poem's painterly qualities, being "Domination of Black." The scene is perhaps a reminiscence of the poet's childhood. The hemlock he refers to is a dark, heavy evergreen commonly planted around homes in the north of the United States as a hedge and wind-break. In Stevens' youth, also, it was not uncommon for a farm in Pennsylvania, where he grew up, to keep a peacock or two in the yard. These details, therefore,

are realistic, not fanciful. The poem, like a Braque painting, is
based on actual objects:

> At night, by the fire,
> The colors of the bushes
> And of the fallen leaves,
> Repeating themselves,
> Turned in the room,
> Like the leaves themselves
> Turning in the wind.
> Yes: but the color of the heavy hemlocks
> Came striding.
> And I remembered the cry of the peacocks.
>
> The colors of their tails
> Were like the leaves themselves
> Turning in the wind,
> In the twilight wind.
> They swept over the room,
> Just as they flew from the boughs of the hemlocks
> Down to the ground.
> I heard them cry—the peacocks.
> Was it a cry against the twilight
> Or against the leaves themselves
> Turning in the wind,
> Turning as the flames
> Turned in the fire,
> Turning as the tails of the peacocks
> Turned in the loud fire,
> Loud as the hemlocks
> Full of the cry of the peacocks?
> Or was it a cry against the hemlocks?
>
> Out of the window,
> I saw how the planets gathered
> Like the leaves themselves
> Turning in the wind.
> I saw how the night came,
> Came striding like the color of the heavy hemlocks
> I felt afraid.
> And I remembered the cry of the peacocks.

In some poems Stevens' intention, though not vague, is at-
mospheric and as "irrational" as music. More often, at least in

his first book, it is specific enough but conveyed by poetic means, image, symbol and sound, rather than by statement. One main key to his work is to realize that like Yeats, though less systematically, he has built up in his poetry a system of symbols, a kind of private language or poetic shorthand, which we can to a degree translate into lines of meaning. The sun, for example, quite regularly stands for reality, the "unthinking source," while the moon presides over the imagination. The colors red and blue have similar opposite connotations. The poet, the man of imagination, is often represented by a performer, a "comedian" or pianist or guitar player. The South is the country of the imagination and Spaniards, the people who are at home in it, while the North is "essential prose" and northerners are realists. These are mere crude notations of the kind of thing to look for; actually, Stevens' symbols are built up within and for each poem, with endless variations, additions, reversals, ironies. The point is that one of his poems helps another, so that the best solution to the problem of reading Stevens is to read him until his special language becomes familiar and transparent.

A final clue to Stevens is that to a great degree he is a reflexive poet, in the sense that the subject of much of his poetry is poetry. Such a preoccupation is a natural one for the kind of poet we have been describing. In his case it does not lead to a barren formalism, but to an impressive modern restatement of the romantic aesthetic. He begins where the romantics did, with the post-Kantian discovery of the necessary contribution of the imagination to all human perception and knowledge. The world we inhabit is one we "half create"; we make the order we perceive. The poet, then, for Stevens (as for Coleridge or Shelley) becomes the archetype of the creative power of thought on which all human understanding depends. Stevens does not, like some romantics, suggest that the human mind can make the world it wills. No poetry is possible without the severe discipline of reality. Stevens' view of man is modern and naturalistic, not the "spilt religion" of the romantics. Like them, however, he asserts the dignity as well as the discipline of the poet. "What makes the poet the potent figure

that he is, or was, or ought to be," he writes, "is that he creates
the world to which we turn incessantly and without knowing
it and that he gives to life the supreme fictions without which
we are unable to conceive of it." "I am," his poet asserts,

> I am the necessary angel of the earth,
> Since, in my sight, you see the earth again.

The same could be said by many other poets of this great
period in American verse.

12: The Larger Audience

"AMERICAN POETRY in these years," wrote F. O. Matthiessen in 1948, "furnished the most serious evidence of a cleavage between what we have learned to call mass civilization and minority culture." As we have seen in previous chapters, the period between the two World Wars reflected, at least in its poetry and criticism, the growth of a minority culture to a high level of sophistication and excellence. Poets like E. E. Cummings, Wallace Stevens, Hart Crane, William Carlos Williams, and Marianne Moore flourished in the mood of analysis, standards, and classical retreat created by the New Criticism, while poets like Robinson Jeffers and Archibald MacLeish had difficulty in finding their places between the mass and the minority.

But much of ultimate importance to literature was happening outside the range of the tower—of structural steel or ivory, be that as it may. The movies had meanwhile learned to talk, the radio had learned to see, and networks of wires and wireless waves made antennae of as much importance to man as to bug. Now for the first time in history, an artist could communicate directly with an audience of 185,000,000 who freely chose to give him their attention or withhold it. What is unusual is that such large-scale communication is possible to someone in whose behalf no compulsion can be exerted, someone who has nothing to sell but his talent or his personality. But, we must note, he has these qualities *to sell*. And so he creates a commodity, something which must be sold and which may or may not be a work of art. Its merit depends on the taste of the mass audience, which is often bad but sometimes good. The mass audience can respond to good things, and we have occasional hopeful signs that the more good things it gets, the more it responds to them.

Our interest in the mass media is threefold.

First, we seek out, examine, and enjoy the best that has been created for the mass audience. We want to appreciate and understand the good film, the good performance, the exciting sports event, and the intelligent news telecast.

Second, we recognize the thousand influences that the mass media have exercised upon our daily lives. We speak a more nearly uniform language because of radio, television, and films. Children, two decades ago, began to eat more spinach because a comic-strip character recommended it. Underwear manufacturers suffered when, in a film, Clark Gable revealed that he wore nothing under his shirt.

Third, the mass media hold mirrors up to us, show us the reflections of the popular mind and the embodiments of the great American myths. As the century began, the widely read fiction of Horatio Alger Jr. dramatized the American dream of success as the reward of virtue. If success now seems more mysterious and less attainable, we not only have serious treatments of this matter in Arthur Miller's *Death of a Salesman* and Saul Bellow's *Seize the Day*, but we also have an appropriate mass myth in the comic-strip story of Superman, who is changed by a sort of magic from a mild nonentity to a man of steel. Interpreting the myths of our mass culture is a favorite practice of many serious critics who are equally capable of writing on highbrow, esoteric art.

The first of the mass media came into being at roughly the same time—the end of the nineteenth century. They were the films and the popular press as we know it. The popular newspapers of the 1890's were called the yellow press, and, significantly, they were so called because one of these papers

ran a comic strip called "The Yellow Kid," which was among
the first modern comics. The next significant development
took place after World War I—the advent of radio and talking
pictures. With the depression of the 1930's came cut-rate entertainment in the form of comic books and paperbacks. The more
prosperous period following World War II has brought us
television and the quality paperback.

The film is still the monarch of our mass media. Movie
studios have long comprised one of America's major indus-
tries, and their products are the chief interpreters of America's
image. The film is not primarily a literary medium, as a thousand facts remind us—the primacy of the image, the dominance
of the director, the star system, the practice of collaboration
among writers who cannot govern the final destiny of the
words they write. And yet Hollywood's great creative artists
are in a sense men of letters, for they have created characters,
plots, images—all but words. The signature of a Chaplin or a
Buster Keaton or a D. W. Griffith or a John Huston is as
distinctive as that of a Fitzgerald or a Faulkner in fiction. I
mention Fitzgerald and Faulkner because they worked for
many years as screen writers. Their writing for the screen was
highly regarded by their employers, but they failed to establish any distinctive quality by which their films might be
known. On the other hand, writers of the second or third rank
apparently did a better job of supplying stories for films—
writers like W. R. Burnett, Clarence Budington Kelland, and
Dashiell Hammett. Who wrote *High Noon*? I confess I do not
know. Why did these minor writers succeed where Fitzgerald
and Faulkner failed? Perhaps because their action was simple
and fundamental, perhaps because their writing was more malle-
able and gave more play to the mind of a Frank Capra or a
John Huston. Capra's most memorable film was probably *Mr.
Deeds Goes to Town*, based on a novel by Kelland. Huston
made his reputation filming novels by Burnett and Hammett.
Hammett's *The Maltese Falcon* has been filmed three times,
but only once was it remarkable on the screen, when it was
directed by Huston.

Many of the most memorable American films show us a

lonely, plucky adventurer facing unknown dangers. This encounter must surely be one of the great American myths. We find it first in the silent films of Charlie Chaplin, Buster Keaton, and Harold Lloyd. Chaplin's tramp is a vindictive but sensitive victim of circumstances. Keaton's character was always glum, and Lloyd's was always eager, but both put their even tempers to the test when they collided with extraordinary events. Later, Frank Capra espoused a typically American tolerance of personal idiosyncrasy. Capra, as in *Mr. Deeds Goes to Town* or in *Mr. Smith Goes to Washington*, usually tells the story of a naïve young man who opposes urbane hypocrisy and triumphs over it. Other resolute heroes have tended to be distinctively American creations—the gangster, the cowboy, and the private detective. Their stories, too, are parables of self-reliance. In *Public Enemy*, *Scarface*, and *Little Caesar*, self-reliance becomes antisocial and is punished, but the film gangster was not a hero for nothing. *The Maltese Falcon* celebrates the private detective; its motto might be that of Melville's confidence man—"No trust." Over the years, the western has surely been the most profitable sort of film. Both trivial and serious western films concern the lonely cowboy hero. Among the serious westerns we might name *High Noon*, *The Gunfighter*, and John Ford's celebrations of forced unions in the face of adversity—a group of films of which *Stagecoach* is a good example.

In each of these films, the lone man or the isolated party confronts a new land, a new experience. Each hero approaches the condition of Chaplin and Keaton, who seem innocent of any previous experience. Life happens to all of them for the first time. Its unseen threats are bewildering, complex, unnerving—Indians in ambush, the consequences of crime, the possibilities of corruption, and even the results of enjoying a reputation as a fast draw.

As for more sophisticated subjects, one has the feeling that American films are still only beginning to explore this new territory. For only a few years has the weakening of self-imposed film censorship permitted full examination of what we call "adult" subjects. But among the adult films we must name one great forerunner, the story of a fabulous American success who was really a child at heart—Orson Welles's *Citizen Kane*. This was our only professionally made talking film in which one man controlled everything; its high quality possibly speaks for the virtue of having one mind control the whole process of filming. Script, performance, and camera work set new standards of excellence. But now, our recent films face up to an odd assortment of serious problems—war, atomic destruction, racial prejudice, juvenile delinquency, drug addiction—and our comedies, too, like *Some Like It Hot* and *The Apartment*, are more knowing.

This new development may reflect an alteration in our national character, but it must also reflect a change in the place the film plays in our lives; it is no longer the ideal entertainment for all the family. That function now belongs to television, which directly enters the home and reaches the whole family group. In competing with television, the new film can now claim greater frankness as one of its selling points. The new film strives also to capture the immediacy of television, showing events as if the camera had caught them accidentally, endeavoring to convey a documentary quality.

But the quality of document belongs legitimately to television, in its sports events, in its political conventions, in its real contestants even when they compete in unreal contests. Obviously, television appeals most of all on the grounds of its reality and immediacy. Its drama, like its special events, possesses the reality of minute details, of accurate sectional accents, of domestic routines and daily chores. Notwithstanding this odd emphasis in television drama, the medium has produced some writers of talent—Paddy Chayefsky, Gore Vidal, William Gibson, Reginald Rose—but few of the best write for it now, and television seems to be awaiting a new generation of dramatists.

The present promise of television lies where the strength of the early silent film lay, in its comedians. Where the silent comedians confronted experience armed only in their native innocence, the television comedians are all-knowing skeptics. I am thinking especially of Phil Silvers, Sid Caesar, and such newer arrivals as Mort Sahl, Shelley Berman, and Nichols and May. Silvers, as Sergeant Bilko, is the confidence man *par excellence*, continuing an American tradition that goes back to Melville and Poe. Caesar has many identities, but he is primarily a parodist, and a parodist must embody not naïveté but superiority to what he parodies—whether it be a foreign movie, an urban husband, or a psychoanalyst. Sahl and Berman give the impression of knowing all the truths of our daily lives, of seeing through them and being superior to them.

No one can yet say what television performances have any lasting importance. Immediate social effect seems limited to the westerns, which are widely imitated by children. The best of the comedians are mainly—perhaps only—for adults. We have no present equivalent for the children's comedians of a generation ago, for Joe Penner, who taught us to say "Ya wanna buy a duck?" or for Eddie Cantor, who taught our human ducklings to go "quack quack quack."

Television, like radio, consumes material insatiably, and without bestowing any permanence. It was perhaps the greatest of radio comedians, Fred Allen, who complained that he was on a "treadmill to oblivion." Allen, a genial parodist, was one of the funniest men who ever lived. And what remains of his accomplishment? Hundreds of recordings which no one now hears and two books. The two important playwriting names that radio produced—Arch Oboler and Norman Corwin—have now receded into relative obscurity. But once in a while a natural talent broke loose, in radio as in the other mass media. The first name to occur is again that of Orson Welles, whose dramatic programs reflected common sense and good taste. Welles unexpectedly became famous when listeners who tuned in late to one of his plays thought we were being invaded from Mars. His unsponsored series had no famous stars; opposite it, on another network, was the most popular program of the time. And yet listeners in great numbers would turn away from this glittering variety show to learn what was happening on Welles's modest program. I can think of no better reason for expressing faith in popular taste, once it has access to quality.

We have still another sort of "speaking" picture in the comic strips—read daily by millions of Americans. Long ago the comics stopped being uniformly comical, and they now furnish our daily ration of fiction. A few possess some verve and originality, and they have influenced our national life. *Krazy Kat* was the favorite of the intellectuals; *Thimble Theatre* introduced Popeye, who ate spinach, and Wimpy, who ate hamburgers; *Mickey Mouse* inaugurated Walt Disney's cartoon industry; and the place of *Li'l Abner* is unique, for it has given us a whole *ersatz* folklore tailored to fit the town of Dogpatch. *Pogo* and *Peanuts*, relatively young strips, are hopeful signs, for they are literate comics that withstand the test of irony.

What has all this to do with literature? Films, television, and the comics have given us a literature conveyed in images as well as words. The wedding seems to be one of those that no man can put asunder because we show little interest in the words alone. Film scripts have been published, but without winning any substantial audience. We ignore the scripts not because we despise our films and prefer to forget them but because the films themselves always remain to be seen again, not in disembodied words but in talking pictures. Yet now, curiously, there exists a limited market for published television plays—perhaps because, unlike film scripts, they are one-man plays, ascribable to single authors, perhaps because television programs are not always available to be seen again, perhaps because everyone feels he can write a television play and needs only to learn to write camera directions.

But words alone have enjoyed a revival in the mass market as well as words with pictures. The quality paperbacks have made serious books available in inexpensive editions. They sell widely, many of them to college students, and many to a public that would never seek these books out in a college library. A recent catalogue of these paperbacks lists 9,100 titles in print, and the number continues to grow. Far from destroying or even discouraging the esoteric writer, the quality paperbacks have given him a larger audience. Among those to profit from this development are such difficult poets as Ezra Pound and

E. E. Cummings and such difficult critics as R. P. Blackmur and Francis Fergusson. New magazines, like the *Evergreen Review*, have burgeoned among the quality paperbacks, and at least one old literary magazine, *Partisan Review*, has become a quality paperback. The result is to foster cultural pluralism and to help to establish those serious standards by which our popular arts may be judged.

13: Theatre Without Walls

AMERICAN DRAMA since the end of World War II has been pushing down walls so that it can find room to stand on a smaller and smaller space. There are two kinds of falling walls involved, those that hold up the Broadway theatres and those that enclose the old-fashioned realistic sets which once ruled beneath the proscenium arch; in many cases even the arch is gone. It is certainly characteristic of American theatre in the last fifteen years that off-Broadway, regional, and university productions have had vitality enough to influence Broadway; also characteristic of the period has been the wide variety of experiments in staging.

The "smaller space" of the above sentence refers to subject matter. For the most part, American playwrights since the war have become increasingly concerned with the individual in close-up; their approach has narrowed the context in which the protagonist moves, seldom allowing him to belong to any group larger than the family. Psychological concerns have won out over social. The typical play of the postwar years is likely to be a study of psychological—probably sexual—problems, staged in a nonrealistic set, perhaps first presented off Broadway, even as far off Broadway as Dallas or Cleveland.

So neat a summation of typicality need not be taken as all-inclusive; there are exceptions that will not fit these limits. Nor should one assume that a description of the postwar theatre implies a declaration that it is new or startling. American theatre went heavily psychological in the twenties and, in the same decade, played seriously with experimental staging; the Broadway theatre has always been sniped at or tempted by some little theatre or other. What follows, then, is not an unveiling of the unexpected; it is an examination of the ways in which the postwar theatre has used and modified the traditional structure, methods and subjects of American theatre and tempered them to the times.

Traditionally, the off-Broadway group was a collection of people who shared a particular aesthetic or social idea and who gathered together so that they might voice that idea in the face of the philistine commercial theatre. The Provincetown Playhouse, for instance, was mainly a playwrights' theatre, a group of men and women who believed that drama could be as serious, and as literary, as the other genres. The footwork of the uptown philistine has always been good, however, and as soon as any group or any idea caught on it was absorbed into the commercial theatre the way third political parties in this country are swallowed by the two major ones.

The unique thing about off-Broadway activity since 1945 is that it has been primarily an economic venture. The off-Broadway groups are more professional than they are revolutionary, and their income is as important to them as their ideals. The commercial side of current off-Broadway activity is immediately apparent if one examines the way in which a play gets onto an off-Broadway stage. There are no longer groups in which the actors and directors are also the producers and managers. There are very few continuing groups at all. One of the apparent exceptions, the Circle in the Square, has been doing solidly effective work ever since its successful revival of Tennessee Williams' *Summer and Smoke* in 1952. Although many actors appear in more than one Circle production, the group is primarily a continuity of management and of direction, since José Quintero is one of the producing triumvirate which controls the organization. For the most part, however, an off-Broadway producer, like his uptown equivalent, finds a play that he likes or that he suspects a large enough group of playgoers will like, and then rents a theatre, assembles a cast, finds a director and a set designer, hires a publicity man, and is in business. That it can be a profitable business, although usually it is not, can be seen from the fact that Broadway producers—Roger L. Stevens for instance— are now moving off Broadway to do certain kinds of plays.

In emphasizing the economic motivation of much of the off-Broadway activity, I do not intend belittling the activity itself. There have been plenty of inferior productions, of course, but on the whole the off-Broadway record of the last ten years is a better one, a more sustained one, than earlier years can show. Off-Broadway's contribution to American theatre, if not to American drama, has been a solid one. It has made available to theatregoers many of the classics of the modern theatre, the works of Ibsen, Strindberg, Chekhov, O'Casey, Lorca, plays which Broadway will not ordinarily risk doing. It has introduced to American audiences still-controversial playwrights—Beckett, Ionesco, Genet, Adamov. It has found virtues in American plays that initial Broadway production failed to show. O'Neill's *The Iceman Cometh*, Williams' *Orpheus Descending*, Truman Capote's *The Grass Harp*, are only three of many plays that have found their audiences through more intimate productions in smaller theatres. Off-Broadway has also turned up a wealth of acting talent, sending performers like Kim Stanley, Jason Robards, Jr., Geraldine Page, Fritz Weaver, and Earle Hyman to the larger audiences of Broadway and the movies; directors, too—most notably Quintero—have had their start off Broadway.

These flourishing small theatres seem to have given us everything except new American plays. There are exceptions, of course. Alfred Hayes's *The Girl on the Via Flaminia*, one of the few genuinely moving plays to come out of the war, and Calder Willingham's *End as a Man*, both began off Broadway. That both plays failed when they moved uptown to larger theatres is a further indication that some plays demand a small theatre and a small audience. It was the recognition of this fact that made Tennessee Williams offer his *Suddenly Last*

Summer for off-Broadway production. Williams is Williams, of course, and even Hayes and Willingham did not come unknown to the theatre, for their plays are adaptations of novels which had already reached audiences of their own. If off-Broadway is to make a real contribution to American drama, it will have to find new playwrights, men who respond to its restrictions and expand in its comparative freedom. In the last few years, new playwrights have begun to appear. Let us hope that Jack Gelber's *The Connection*, Edward Albee's *The Zoo Story* and *The American Dream*, and Jack Richardson's *The Prodigal* are only the beginning.

If one needed a metaphor, it might be possible to consider off-Broadway theatre as the little brother of Broadway, a brother not so rich or so well dressed, but one much more inquisitive and, probably, rather more intelligent. Once metaphors get in, however, there is no holding them. Regional theatre, then, is likely to become the country cousin who, on closer look, turns out to be more sophisticated than the city cousin, and university theatre might become a distant relative, conservative for the most part, but capable of mouth-watering eccentricities. Although Broadway pretends to ignore these poor relatives, it will borrow from them anything—play, playwright, actor, director, staging technique—that has been tried and found workable.

The word "regional" in the phrase "regional theatre," however, does not imply the limitations of subject matter, the self-conscious sense of place that we ordinarily mean when we speak of regional literature. It refers to those theatres that flourish outside of New York City—for example, in San Francisco, Los Angeles, Cleveland, Dallas, Houston, Topeka, Milwaukee, Philadelphia. Nor does it refer to the summer theatres, mostly pale imitations of Broadway; nor the amateur groups who have a fondness for last year's New York comedy hit. The regional theatre is made up of those professional or semiprofessional groups which make an effort to bring to American cities all across the country the solidity of good theatre classics and new plays. The existence of such groups is often precarious; they form and disappear; the quality of their work goes up and down, often depending on who runs which group what year. At their best, they have an influence far beyond the cities in which they operate.

The theatre that the late Margo Jones ran in Dallas is a good example; it was particularly friendly to new plays and new playwrights. In its first season—in the summer of 1947—it not only introduced Tennessee Williams' newest play, *Summer and Smoke*, but it also introduced a new playwright, William Inge, whose offering, *Farther Off From Heaven*, was to be rewritten more than ten years later as *The Dark at the Top of the Stairs*. After Miss Jones's death in 1955, the theatre bearing her name continued, but without her personality to mold it, its influence beyond the edge of the city was small. Today, theatre people all across the country are again looking toward Dallas, waiting to see what will be made of the new Dallas Theater Center. Part school, part repertory, housed in a Frank Lloyd Wright theatre, the Center is under the direction of Paul Baker, whose productions at Baylor University had already attracted attention beyond the borders of Texas.

The importance of such regional theatres to American drama has finally been recognized by the Ford Foundation, a recognition that may free at least some of them to work without creditors breathing down their necks. In 1960, the Alley Theatre in Houston, the Actor's Workshop in San Francisco, and the Phoenix Theatre in New York, having found donations to match generous grants from the foundation, plan to operate with full-time repertory companies. The Arena Stage in Washington, to which Ford has made the same dollar-for-dollar offer, will probably follow suit.

The university theatres have also made their contribution to American drama. It is true that many of them lack either the facilities or the imagination to try new things, but there are happy exceptions. F. Curtis Canfield's group at Yale first produced Archibald MacLeish's *J.B.*, and later performed it in the American Theatre at the World's Fair in Brussels. The activity at Harvard, at least until the opening of the new theatre center there, has lacked any controlling hand, but out of its diversity has come, most recently, a playwright as imaginative as Arthur

L. Kopit. Kopit's play *Oh Dad, Poor Dad, Mamma's Hung You in the Closet and I'm Feelin' So Sad*, an Ionesco-like variation on an American theme, galloping momism, was first done by one of the undergraduate groups.

Let's turn now from the falling wall of the Broadway theatre to the falling wall of the realistic set. Recently Celeste Holm, making a guest appearance on a TV show, said that she had acted in the round, in the three-quarter round, and in the semicircle, and that she was looking for some new shape to try. Her joking remark has point only because the American theatre has been so busily trying so many forms in the years since the war. Glenn Hughes at the University of Washington developed theatre-in-the-round during the thirties for his Penthouse Theatre, but it was not until the late forties that this kind of production, in which the audience completely surrounds the actors, really became popular. Little theatres and university theatres took to it because it simplified some problems of sets and housing. One of the reasons for the commercial experiments, like the one at the Edison Hotel in New York, was that the collapse of the night club business right after the war left vacant rooms that could be easily and inexpensively converted into theatres-in-the-round.

The dramatic advantage of this kind of production, so its adherents say, is that it provides a communication between the audience and the actors that the proscenium arch necessarily destroys. When the play is right and the actors are right, this exchange does take place, but for some playwrights—Ibsen, say, or Shaw—the round is as incongruous as the tight proscenium is for Shakespeare. Theatre-in-the-round, then, was not really the theatrical panacea that it seemed to be to Margo Jones when she wrote her book about it in 1951. Almost as soon as the form became popular it began to be modified; the Circle in the Square, for instance, was never a circle. Its three-quarter round became the most workable variation on the not-quite-perfect circle. The complete round found its happiest use in the music tents which now dot the country, where summer audiences mix the pleasure of musical comedy with the fun of the circus.

More important, finally, than the fact of theatre-in-the-round is the attitude of mind that was drawn to it. While the round-heads were calling spectators into circles, other producers were pushing out toward the audience, using aprons, runways, platforms, all the devices that could help break down the invisible fourth wall between audience and actor. This manipulation of the size and shape of the stage had its counterpart in set design. In the years immediately after the war, plays like *Death of a Salesman* and *A Streetcar Named Desire* demanded and got sets that were more suggestive than realistic. In *Salesman,* for instance, Jo Mielziner's imaginative, multilevel design allowed the characters to step not only from room to room, but from year to year, from dream to dream. It looked then as though the expressionistic techniques of the twenties were being domesticated to suit a new kind of American play, one that tempered its realism by mood and symbol.

Lately, there has been a reaction—an unfortunate one, I think. The vigor and inventiveness of American set-making of the late forties has given way, on the one hand to a kind of nervous gadgetry, represented by Mielziner's set for *Sweet Bird of Youth,* and on the other to the old-fashioned, photographic realism of a set like Ralph Alswang's apartment for *A Raisin in the Sun.* If the hopes of the *Salesman* days are a little dampened, if there is the possibility now that we will not be able to hold on to the simplicity that tries to achieve the feel of correctness through hint and suggestion, there is at least no longer the necessity for the American playwright and his designer to feel trapped by the dictatorial single set. The play, now, if the subject demands it, can be as free and fluid as the musical comedy; there is, in fact, good reason to suspect that the staging and design of musicals has been one of the formative influences on the relaxation of realism on the American stage.

Television, strangely, has been another such influence. Although television drama has been most determinedly realistic, the realism of that medium is not necessarily the realism of the theatre. Television plays are constructed by tiny scenes, and the production snakes through a series of minuscule sets in which the actors have space to perform only the smallest, the briefest action. Transfer this method to the stage, and what was essentially realistic becomes artificial, stylized in set and lighting. Even a studiously conventional play—William Gibson's *The Miracle Worker*, for instance—is likely to have a great deal of fluidity; the author does not hesitate to allow himself short scenes, quick changes of time and place, simultaneous actions on stage. Multiple sets, moving sets, spotlighting, a wide range of theatrical devices are at the playwright's service, but part of the desire to use them so extensively comes from an attempt to approximate on stage the television play's flexibility. That so many contemporary playwrights—Paddy Chayefsky, Richard Nash, Gore Vidal, Shimon Wincelberg—are also television playwrights only emphasizes these similarities.

Although the television play uses a kind of openness of structure, there is ordinarily a closeness of subject matter. The sense of containment implicit in the method of production, the need to focus on a single character, or on a tight group of characters, forces the television writer to a consideration of individual problems. The psychological play, then, rather than the social one, became the standard for television drama. It has also been the standard for the theatre in the last dozen years.

Although I have suggested a cause-effect relationship between television and the theatre in the matter of structure and staging, I intend no relationship stronger than an analogous one in subject matter. It is probably true that the success of live television drama in the early fifties fed a tendency which was already evident on stage; it is certainly true that those writers who came from television to Broadway brought with them an allegiance to the kind of play they had been doing for the small screen. The important thing, however, was that the postwar American stage had already embraced the psychological play with an enthusiasm not seen since the twenties when Freud finally filtered through to Broadway.

In the years immediately after the war there were a number of plays in which context shared the spotlight with character, plays like William Wister Haines's *Command Decision*, but

even then the American stage had ceased to be overtly concerned with social problems. There was a rash of plays on
Negro-white relations—*Deep Are the Roots* by Arnaud d'Us-
seau and James Gow, for example—but these were only implicitly social plays; concerned, as they so often were, with
miscegenation, they became variations of standard domestic
plays, preferring private passions to public problems. A typical
play of the early postwar years is Arthur Laurents' *Home of
the Brave.* Produced in 1945, it came close enough to the
thirties to be concerned with so societal a problem as anti-
Semitism, but it looked to the fifties by treating the problem
in purely psychological terms.

The average play of the fifties concerns itself with the problems of adjustment, of acceptance. The protagonist, often
enough, is put into a family situation where his wife, his
parent, his child becomes the antagonist and drives him to or
saves him from alcoholism, homosexuality, mental breakdown,
drug addiction, or simple boredom. In the absence of family,
a love affair or a courtship can serve as tension builder and
reliever. The solution, often enough, is sexual, the copulative
salvation of the hero through benign interference; the most
famous example, of course, is Robert Anderson's *Tea and
Sympathy* in which the master's wife saves the student from
incipient homosexuality by offering her body as therapy. Also,
much of the dialogue in the average play is likely to be in the
clichés of psychological jargon, and the general tone is inevitably didactic.

American playwrights have always been teachers and reformers; in the postwar years, with the social play no longer popular, the playwright has become a kind of marriage counselor,
insisting that love, by which he usually means sex, conquers
all. Consider, for instance, the end of William Inge's *The Dark
at the Top of the Stairs.* After sprinkling the stage with every
complication from infidelity to anti-Semitism, Inge smooths
away all difficulties by sending Rubin Flood and his wife up
the stairs, hand in hand. Earlier in the play, Inge has given the
audience an endlessly explicit object lesson in the figure of
Mrs. Flood's sister, a comic-pathetic character who cannot quit

talking about her frigidity and what it has done to her marriage and her life. Inge, who masks his sentimental bromides in the lineaments of seriousness, is probably the most representative playwright of the fifties, and *The Dark at the Top of the Stairs*, in which psychological drama is finally reduced to the level of the newspaper advice column, is not only his most typical, but also his most popular play.

Even a play like Paddy Chayefsky's *The Tenth Man*, for all its surface difference, is very much a part of the Inge-Anderson-Laurents pattern. Despite the pseudo-Yiddish comedy involved in the search for a *minyan* and the ambiguous use of mysticism in the presentation of a *dybbuk*, Chayefsky's play is little more than the decision of the two tortured young people to share their pain, to try out the curative powers of that very popular antibiotic, *love*. Of course, anyone who had seen Chayefsky's *Middle of the Night* or his earlier television plays was not surprised to find in him more psychology than supernaturalism.

Comedy, for the most part, has been remarkably like the serious drama in the years since the war. High comedy, which was never really domesticated in America, except obliquely in some of the plays of S. N. Behrman and Philip Barry, has practically disappeared, except for the trickles evident in a play like Samuel Taylor's *The Pleasure of His Company*. Gone, too, is the more genuinely American comedy, the tough-sentimental play like those of Kaufman and Hart. Right after the war it looked as though Garson Kanin, with *Born Yesterday*, might carry on that tradition, but he moved it to Hollywood in movies as good as *The Marrying Kind*, and it died out there. It exists now only in musical comedies like *Guys and Dolls*, but even these have to fight for stage space with the more ambitious musical plays and with the American variation on the European operetta, shows like the Lerner and Loewe *My Fair Lady*.

Satirical comedy—particularly political satire—has almost completely disappeared. The only play with a tough satirical spine to it to turn up in the last few years is Gore Vidal's pacifist farce *Visit to a Small Planet* and that, ironically, is an expanded version of a television play. There have been any number of plays, none worth remembering, that kid safe targets like suburban conformity, and there have been highly successful farces like *Anniversary Waltz*, by Joseph Fields and Jerome Chodorov, in which the high point comes when the hero kicks in the front of a television set.

Perhaps the most typical comedy of the period is William Gibson's *Two for the Seesaw*, but it would be very difficult to tell it from the average serious play. It is true that there are a great number of supposedly funny lines, built as often as not on the assumption that a mild swear word is a sure laugh-catcher, and the heroine has a vague, long-distance relation to the tradition of the pathetic comic hero. But the play is mainly a bittersweet concoction, a long look at a love affair between a mismatched couple, each trying to damp down his loneliness. When they part at the end of the play, they are richer, fuller, stronger for the experience—education in the Inge tradition. Sadly, Tennessee Williams, who has a real talent for grotesque comedy, has written a play not unlike Gibson's in *Period of Adjustment*, although there is a saving suspicion of irony about the whole thing.

Of all the American playwrights of the period since World War II, Tennessee Williams and Arthur Miller alone have any claim to the laurels of the major dramatist. The final validity of their claims will not be known for at least another fifty years, but Miller's chances of holding on to those laurels are rather better than Williams'. In any case, neither of them fits comfortably into a generalization about the drama of this period, the way Inge or Gibson does. Still, for all their individual qualities, they are also a part of their own time.

Williams, for instance, is very much a part of the contemporary concern with psychological problems, although he uses them to suit his own purposes. His protagonists suffer from frustration and loneliness, as do those of most contemporary playwrights, but, except in *Period of Adjustment* and *The Rose Tattoo*, he makes no attempt at a solution. He is enough a part of his own time to have a yearning for the healthy, the average, the adjusted. This is clear even in *A Streetcar Named*

Desire, where his ambiguous attitude to Stanley, the destroyer, saves the play from those black-and-white interpretations which range Blanche against Stanley as good against evil.

There is no doubt, however, that Williams is attracted to the Blanches, the victims of this world. The protagonists of almost all of his plays are outsiders, separated from the ordinary world by sensibility (Blanche), purity (Val Xavier in *Orpheus Descending*) or glittering corruption (the dead poet in *Suddenly Last Summer*). These outsiders come to embody art and religion, all the inspiriting virtues which make man potentially greater than he is, which Williams makes clear both in his conscious use of myth in the later plays and in the symbolizing tendency of his caricatures in the earlier ones. These outsiders must finally be destroyed by a society in which "mendacity," to borrow the key word from *Cat on a Hot Tin Roof*, is preferable to the grand lies of art and imagination, where self-seeking has replaced that beautiful and ineffectual quality, *pity*.

The seeds of Willaims' own destruction lie in his excessively romantic vision. The grand gestures of his protagonists and the violence of their ends lead him to embrace melodrama, and the line between the melodramatic and the funny is a thin one. His own real gift for comic caricature only complicates the problem. It is impossible to take the poet in *Suddenly Last Summer* seriously; Sebastian may be a saint in name, but the glimpse that we get of him through the mouth of his mother suggests broad satire. The man who goes in search of God and collects small boys is the ascetic as aesthete; the poet with his one perfect poem a year is the ultimate of the amateur in art. Whether the implicit satire in *Suddenly Last Summer* is accidental or intentional, that play displays the difficulty with Williams, the problem of balance between the comedian of *Baby Doll* and the melodramatist of *Streetcar*. In any case, it has become increasingly obvious in the last few years that Williams is not a playwright of ideas. All that he has to communicate is his own sensibility, his almost visceral feeling of horror at the world, which he describes in *Period of Adjustment* as a vast neurasthenic ward. The question is whether or not the sensibility is giving way to the gesture that represents it.

Arthur Miller, like Williams, is both part of and greater than his moment in the history of American drama. His plays, like those of his contemporaries, focus on a small segment of human conflict, but Miller never confuses the segment with the whole. All of his plays—even *The Crucible*—are domestic dramas that use the family as the testing place for the protagonist. Yet Miller, who is as much a social playwright as he is a psychological one, insists on placing the family in context, insists on the societal concepts that form and distort the family and the individual.

Miller's strength as a playwright, however, does not lie in his obvious ability to give his characters flesh; it lies in the central concern that informs his work. The protagonists of all his plays are forced to see themselves clearly, a recognition that sometimes proves fatal, sometimes triumphant. In each case the individual is in conflict with a societal image by which he may be judged. Joe Keller in *All My Sons* and Willy Loman in *Death of a Salesman* have accepted American myths, the first concerning the primacy of family, the second concerning the importance of success, and have been destroyed by their acceptance; Willy, it is true, learns before his death that there are alternatives. John Proctor in *The Crucible* and Eddie Carbone in *A View from the Bridge* are both concerned about their names—that is, their dignity as men; the first saves his name and the second loses his by the same act, the rejection of the conformity demanded by his society. It is obvious, in *The Crucible*, for instance, that Miller has a strong sense of the rightness or wrongness of the images society forces on its members, but he is primarily concerned, in play after play, with the protagonist's need to separate himself from the wrong images and to find the right.

Only on the surface are Miller and Williams psychological playwrights in the current vogue. Their preoccupation with the individual is closer to that of the world's major playwrights than it is to that of their contemporaries, who seem to have turned their attention inward, not so much to find understand-

ing in a little space as to avoid confusion in the world of large
ideas. In the years since the end of the war the changes in the
means of production and the methods of staging have brought
easy acceptance of what was once experimental. Although
these changes have made great holes in the restrictive walls of
the realistic theatre, only a very few American playwrights
have dared to break through, to go out and up. What we
need at the moment are playwrights willing to risk a great
deal. Perhaps we have a theatre without walls; what we need
now is a theatre without bounds.

R. W. B. LEWIS

14: Recent Fiction: *Picaro* and Pilgrim

AMERICAN FICTION since World War II has been rich enough in quantity, but its quality has been somewhat puzzling and contradictory. There have been more novels of clear artistic competence than in any previous fifteen-year period; but we are not able to discern among them the decisive power of a Faulkner, or a Hemingway, or even a Scott Fitzgerald—as one *could* discern the stature of those writers fifteen years, say, after the appearance of their own first work. The competence of the present fictional generation is admirable in its way, and it suggests how much of the narrative accomplishments of Faulkner and the others has been studied and absorbed; how much of what they originally gained, through their experiments in form and language and narrative rhythm, has been consolidated and is now a staple native resource. The younger writers have obviously gone to school; but in too many cases they have never left school. Often, indeed, they have quite literally stayed on in the universities of their choice, still studying Faulkner and emulating him, teaching literature to a generation younger yet, and teaching what in America is rather oddly called "creative writing." But little that is genuinely creative seems to come from these courses, except ever more competent works, carefully made, knowingly written, but self-protective and generally lifeless.

Meanwhile, however, a different kind of novel has begun to show up; different and yet no less traditional in its special way. This kind represents what is best in postwar American fiction. It tends, as against the work of mere emulative competence, to be seemingly loose in form, to be episodic and even bumpy in construction, with a good deal of ragged life in it and a fresh set of literary affinities. Within this genre, too, we detect no Faulkner and no Hemingway; perhaps we should not expect to. But the names we do mark out for honor have kept the art of fiction alive in America during hard artistic times, by doing what far greater novelists than they have always done: giving us at once a recognizable picture of the vital confusions of contemporary life, and a provisional form (a fictional form) whereby some vital significance may be discovered within these confusions. Among the names that deserve some honor, I shall mention especially the following: Saul Bellow, J. D. Salinger, Ralph Ellison, Jack Kerouac, James Purdy, and Norman Mailer; and I shall have something to say about each of them.

There are, of course, extreme variations among these writers. They come from different parts of the country and from different backgrounds; they include Jew and Protestant, Negro and white, urbanite and back-countryman. Their work exhibits a great variety of surface subject matter, of emphasis, of intention, and of tone. Like the ablest writers in any American generation, they evince a sort of stubborn idiosyncrasy; unlike their counterparts in a characteristic European generation, they cannot easily be drawn together under a single defining label. But in their case, a stubborn idiosyncrasy is, paradoxically, one of the elements they have most strongly in common; it is, to a great extent, what their novels are exactly about, what their central characters and what they, as authors, most determinedly aim at. Their novels show an openness to experience, a deliberate vulnerability to life, along with a sense of restlessness and a sharp but oddly unspecified urgency. It is as though these novelists, and the characters they create, had been shaken loose by the amount and the violence of the history America has passed through (America, it must be remembered, has until late been unaccustomed to history). But at the same time, the world their created characters move through is a very queer combination indeed of chaos and conformity—a chaos of cultural foundations shaken, and a conformity which is the regular answer of the weak in heart to the experience of chaos. Both phenomena, chaos and conformity, are the great enemies of the thing the best of our postwar writers have especially prized: namely, what Walt Whitman called "personalism" and what he defined eloquently as "the principle of individuality, the pride and centripetal isolation of a human being in himself—identity—personalism." If I call such personalism a stubborn idiosyncrasy, it is because a genuine stubbornness is required for individuality these days; and the individuality arrived at and clung to is likely to appear as pure idiosyncrasy in the heavy-lidded gaze of the conformists.

It is appropriate to quote Walt Whitman in this context. For one of the most striking aspects of Bellow and Salinger and their contemporaries has been their instinct to return, for artistic aid and sustenance, to certain of the great nineteenth-century writers: Whitman himself, but equally Mark Twain and Herman Melville. Bellow and Salinger have been attracted most of all to the slippery heroism and the colloquial rhythms of *Huckleberry Finn;* and Salinger's sixteen-year-old Holden Caulfield (in *The Catcher in the Rye*) is in particular a latter-day Huck, an urbanized and upper-class Huck with money in his pocket—but still, like Huck, an adolescent on the run, confronting again the shocks and temptations of life with the same mixture of naïveté and shrewdness and profound, ineradicable faith. Ralph Ellison has found rather in Melville the dark and vigorous disorder that is his own view of modern experience; and he has found there, too, the large intensive symbolism with which to express his view. Jack Kerouac and Norman Mailer have returned to the ever-expanding spirit, at once visionary and sensual, of Walt Whitman. Indeed, one of Whitman's most famous poems—"Song of the Open Road" —virtually provides the title, as it plainly provides the impetus to Kerouac's best-known work of fiction: *On the Road*.

As a matter of fact, several other of the novels on my brief list might with sufficient accuracy be called *On the Road*. And the fact is, further, that if the contemporary novelists have gone back for inspiration to Whitman and Melville and Mark Twain, it is because they could discover there above everything else paradigm, even archetypal native versions of the sense of experience in our postwar period: of experiences as life on the road; life as a sometimes haphazard journey out and along a far, treacherous, and promising open road whose end is beyond any man's sight; a journey possible only for those who retain a vulnerable openness *to* experience. And in Whitman, Twain, and Melville, too, the contemporaries could see enacted that essential quality, that personalism, that freedom, that is—in the contemporary novel—either the journey's prerequisite or its almost sacred purpose.

It is the choice of *journey* as the representative action in their novels that accounts, in great part, for the relative looseness of construction already referred to. The novels of Bellow and the others are episodic in nature, strung out along a series of frequently quite unconnected human encounters. In a broad meaning of the old word, these are picaresque novels —as indeed, was *Huckleberry Finn;* and as, when looked at in the present perspective, was Walt Whitman's "Song of Myself." They are narratives in a comic vein, relating the random adventures of certain energetic young men on their travels.

I do not mean to suggest that the most impressive postwar fiction in America is without exception picaresque. Several writers of undoubted talent have continued in the more traditional way to explore in depth a particular and fixed situation or community, to deal in the traditional manner not with extensive journeys but with intensive intrigues, with the formation and dissolution of relationships within a closed human network. Such was the method of James Jones in his rough, powerful story of military and erotic intrigue at an American army base, *From Here to Eternity*. It is the method, amid very different tonalities, of the highly accomplished William Styron, in his picture of the dark entanglements of society in the American South, *Lie Down in Darkness.*

This is the typical method, too, of Norman Mailer, both in his overrated and overwritten novel about men at war in the Pacific, *The Naked and the Dead,* and in his less known but more authentic shorter tale, *The Barbary Coast,* the action of which is limited to the tensions and aberrations of a small and insignificant boardinghouse in Brooklyn. But I have included Mailer on the list of representative and hence of picaresque writers exactly because he is the exception that proves the rule. The one work of Mailer that really fulfills his immense promise is not a novel at all. It is a volume called *Advertisements for Myself* (published in 1959): a sort of literary autobiography, a chronologically arranged series of random entries, private memoirs, literary critiques, journalistic essays and bits and pieces of novels abandoned or to come. And whereas in the books that are technically fiction, Mailer is more traditional and less satisfactory, in *Advertisements for Myself* he is overtly picaresque, and in being so finds the form his exceptional abilities needed. In his autobiographical account of the energetic young seeker passing through a number of often disconnected experiences and encounters (chiefly on the disorderly literary scene of New York), we are confronted again with a narrative at least analogous to that of Kerouac's *On the Road.* And indeed, Mailer's own title-phrase is as intentional an echo of Whitman as the phrase of Kerouac; Mailer is reminding us of Whitman's long poem, "Song of Myself."

But if *Advertisements for Myself* and *On the Road,* along with the major novels of Saul Bellow, Ralph Ellison, J. D. Salinger, and James Purdy are picaresque in the broad sense of being episodic tales of random journeys, they are also picaresque in the narrower sense. They focus on the adventures of persons who in some way or other are *picaros:* that is, rogues, outlaws. They seem to us at odds with the institutions and habits of modern middle-class society; they are individuals whom the average conventional and law-abiding citizen would regard with distrust and bewilderment. They may be literally lawbreakers, like the car thieves of Bellow and Kerouac; or like the nameless hero of Ellison's *Invisible Man*, who agitates briskly for a subversive political organization. Or they may be spiritual outlaws, persons whose defining quality is an inability or unwillingness to behave according to the strict moral and social code of the day: like Salinger's sensitive and defiant schoolboy-on-the-run, or the titular hero of James Purdy's *Malcolm*—a singular youth who does not so much defy conventions as remain blissfully innocent about them.

Such a plethora of outlaws, whether literal or spiritual, constitutes a plain enough comment on the times—as those times strike the view of the contemporary novelists, anyhow. Quite evidently, they are skeptical about the values publicly adhered to, the institutions publicly cherished and the conduct publicly accepted by the majority of their fellow Americans. But two points are to be noted. In the first place, the prevailing tone of the contemporary picaresque novel is decidedly comic; and the picaresque characters themselves are not crusaders, they are not tragic or self-sacrificial heroes, they are not reformers; they are much rather Charlie Chaplin types, comedians on the move, at once ridiculous and touching in their defiant roguishness. And in the second place, they are not merely rogues and rebels. They emerge, finally, as pilgrims, too: journeying through a mysterious and hostile world, a world both chaotic and conformist, on their various eccentric pilgrimages—toward some shrine of honor and value and belief. The shrine, in these novels, usually remains out of sight; but it does give a sense of purpose—though purpose undisclosed—to their encounters; and it does give a sense of form—though form not always fulfilled—to the novels these *pícaros* inhabit.

It is because his men-of-the-road evince the least degree of purpose that Jack Kerouac's novels have the least achieved form, and so have the least decisive literary quality of the works on our list. This is perhaps what Norman Mailer meant in *Advertisements for Myself* when he said about Kerouac that, though he has an enormous energy and an "ecstatic" love of language, he nonetheless "lacks discipline, intelligence and a sense of the novel." The energy is everywhere in *On the Road*, and it is the ecstasy that lends to that energy an aura of the sacred; this was the book that not only established the now famous word "beat," but which associated it (in however unpersuasive a manner) with beatitude, or the sacred state of blessedness. But even the young men and women who undertake the frantic journeys, who drink the red wine and dance and make love as they scamper back and forth across the country, from New York to San Francisco: even they express the elaborate pointlessness of their activities. The one and noble function of the time, says one of them, is simply and purely to *move*. And the narrator recalls that, "All alone in the night, I had my own thoughts and held the car to the white line of the holy road. What was I doing? Where was I going?" This ecstatic lack of direction is attributed not only to the persons in the story, but to America itself. "Whither goest thou, America," asks the hero oracularly, "in *thy* shiny car in the night?"

A similar questioning tone pervades Saul Bellow's *The Adventures of Augie March*, but this robust and expansive novel manages—somewhat paradoxically—to create a sense of positive purpose through the very force of repeated negation. Part of Bellow's artistic strength comes from his cunning fusion of Anglo-American literary traditions with Yiddish traditions; and Augie March is what is known in Yiddish folklore as a *schlemazl*—that is, the comic victim of a series of misadventures. But through them all, Augie persists in saying "No" to the temptations that beset him. The persons he meets (in Chicago, in Mexico, in the Pacific during the war) are constantly trying to get possession of him: to recruit him to their cause, to convert him to their beliefs, to adopt him as their son or procure him as their husband. Augie squirms his way out of these occasions because, though he cannot give exact name and shape to his own private holy grail, he can recognize and refuse all false or inadequate versions of it. In a world demoniacally eager to recruit, Augie March is the unrecruitable man; and for all the comic scrapes he gets into, he retains what Whitman called "the pride and centripetal isolation of a human being in himself." A man named Einhorn sums it up when he says to Augie: "All of a sudden I catch on to something about you. You've got *opposition* in you." And this was true, Augie reflects; "I did have the opposition in me, and great desire to offer resistance and to say '*No!*' "

The world tries to recruit young Holden Caulfield, too, in Salinger's *The Catcher in the Rye,* as Holden wanders for three days and nights through the chaos and conformity of New York City. And this loose-limbed and slangy adolescent is as agile as was Augie March at escaping the insinuating tentacles of those who would grab hold of him—whether prostitute or conventional socialite, bartender or schoolteacher. But oddly enough, Salinger's uncertain fledgling has a clearer notion of his life's real desire than do the older and more self-assertive heroes of Bellow and Kerouac; and mainly because *his* desire is not restricted to hanging on to his private identity. It is, rather, the life of compassion. Shuffling and self-deprecating, Holden describes his notion (to his sister Phoebe) as a kind of recurring dream. "I keep picturing all these little kids," he says, "playing some game in this big field of rye and all. Thousands of little kids, and nobody's around—nobody big, I mean—except me. And I'm standing on the edge of some crazy cliff. What I have to do, I have to catch everybody if they start to go over the cliff—I mean if they're running and they don't look where they're going I have to come out from somewhere and *catch* them. That's all I'd do all day. I'd just be the catcher in the rye and all. I know it's crazy, but that's the only thing I'd really like to be." Holden nearly goes over the crazy cliff himself on a number of occasions; but we feel that he does fulfill his ambition, he does become the catcher in the rye.

That note of compassion, of an active involvement with others, is relatively rare in contemporary American fiction, as it has been in American fiction traditionally. The customary American response to the dilemmas of experience has been an emphasis on personalism, on the centripetal isolation of the human self—as the most valiant aspiration in a world of chaotic disruption and conformist grabbing. We return to that aspiration in James Purdy's *Malcolm*, in which one character angrily tells another to "keep your hands off my soul!" And we see it enacted in the ending of Ralph Ellison's *Invisible Man*, when his Negro narrator suddenly abandons his long effort to improve the human lot by collective political effort and seizes the opportunity—during a violent race riot in New York's Harlem—to plunge down into an open manhole, and to remain underground, hibernating and entirely on his own resources, meditating the total, bitterly comic collapse of his high socialistic hopes.

On the other hand, both *Malcolm* and *Invisible Man* make up, so to speak, for their rejection of so much of contemporary life by the way both books identify and then explore the most significant aspects of that life. Both Purdy and Ellison (in their exceedingly different ways) introduce their comically ill-equipped young heroes not merely to assorted individuals and situations, but rather to individuals and situations that are clearly representative of the great sources of power and control in our epoch. In the case of *Malcolm*—a startlingly original novel that verges on ironic allegory—the persons encountered stand, respectively, for Art, for Money, for Religion (or, better, Religiosity), for Sex, for Fate, and for Death. Ralph Ellison, working a larger canvas, keeps his protagonist running through extraordinarily jumbled situations that reveal the contemporary force of race, of education, of technology, of sex, and of politics. In both books, there is a kind of logical order to the elements encountered, and so a pattern of sorts within the experiences undergone. It is not a fixed and final design, and it is, in any case, a design darkly tinged with irony. It serves to explain the fatalities of the hero by making manifest the irrelevance of moral commitment—irrelevance, at least, to the contemporary sources of power and control. But that manifestation only makes the moral commitment of these comic heroes, and implicitly of their authors, all the more compelling. And in their handling of these paradoxical affairs, writers like James Purdy and Ralph Ellison reveal how, even in a world in which the moral order has succumbed to the disruptive and

the possessive, fiction can still achieve that narrative order—
that internal artistic order which is *form*, and on which the
life of fiction must always depend. Conversely, through the
form and order they have created by their narrative art, we
ourselves are able better to measure the disorders of the actual
world we must, somehow, continue to live in.

15: Poetry, Raw or Cooked?

ONE OF the best contemporary American poets of the middle generation, Robert Lowell, has asked whether poetry should be raw or cooked. Inevitably, since his poetry is carefully wrought, he comes out on the side of poetry which is cooked. Yet the notion has got around—and it has spread to England and the Continent—that the most interesting poetry being written in America at the present time is of the raw variety. I do not believe this is true, but before I can establish my case, I must glance backward to the state of poetry in America immediately after World War II.

For a number of reasons poetry lost ground in the years between 1945 and 1955. The paperback revolution greatly increased the sale of fiction, good and bad. In the paperback racks in supermarkets and drugstores there was almost no poetry to be seen. The older publishing houses which had always had a few volumes of verse in their lists, as items of prestige if nothing else, all but deserted the poets. It became extremely difficult for a young poet to place his first volume of verse. There was also a dearth of little magazines to compare with the avant-garde magazines of the 1920's, such as *Broom* and *Secession,* which had published much of the verse of that generation of poets. Because the achievements of T. S. Eliot,

Ezra Pound, Allen Tate, John Crowe Ransom, W. H. Auden, and E. E. Cummings were great, it seemed to many that poetry had come to a dead end, as these older poets consolidated their reputations. What did the newer poets, Delmore Schwartz, Karl Shapiro, Randall Jarrell, John Berryman, and Robert Lowell, and their still younger colleagues, Richard Wilbur, William Meredith, Reed Whittemore, and Louis O. Coxe, have to offer beyond what their distinguished elders had accomplished? With these strikes against the poets of the postwar decade, it looked as if the writing of poetry might become the avocation of a few coterie writers. The scene was very bleak indeed.

In the mid-fifties the situation, mysteriously, began to change. The old-line publishers became more hospitable to poetry. Some of the university presses, which have generally published only scholarly books, issued volumes of verse. Two of them, Indiana and Wesleyan, followed the example of the Yale University Press and established series of younger poets. In 1954 Charles Scribner's Sons began issuing its *Poets of Today* volumes, with the work of three new poets handsomely presented in each annual volume. While New Directions and Alan Swallow continued to stand by the avant-garde poets, as they had for many years, new ventures in the publishing of poetry began to spring up all over the country—Grove Press, Motive Press, Origin Press, Divers Press, Golden Quill Press, Hearse Press, the Pocket Poets Series, issued by City Lights Books in San Francisco, the Jargon Books, issued by Jonathan Williams of Highland, North Carolina, and many others. The "press," in some instances, might be nothing more than a mimeographing machine, but the youngest poets had at least found the means of getting their verse into the light of day.

At about the same time, little magazines devoted to the publishing of poetry began to flourish again. A single issue of *Poetry* magazine (July 1959) reported on the arrival of four such ventures: *Inscape* (Albuquerque, New Mexico); *The San Francisco Review; The Half Moon* (Woodside, Long Island); and *Penny Poems*, whose editors in New Haven ambitiously promised a one-page issue every day, five days a week.

Many of the poets published by these new presses and magazines were beat poets or beatniks, as they have been willing to be called. How does one know a beat poet? Certainly he is avant-garde, though in what direction he is advancing is often difficult to tell. He is in revolt from society but his rebellion has no political tinge because he scorns all social institutions. He demands for himself the utmost personal freedom and he writes as he pleases, usually in the freest of free verse. He lives for emotional kicks, seeking them, if need be, by means of alcohol, sexual experimentation, and dope. He prefers the company of Negroes because Negroes are supposed to be more uninhibited than white men can ever expect to be. He consorts with jazz-men because jazz provides the ultimate apocalyptic vision. He dedicates his poems to William Carlos Williams or to the other hero of all the beats, the novelist Jack Kerouac, born in Lowell, Massachusetts, and on the road ever since.

"Beat" has at least three meanings. It may signify the at-the-bottom stratum of society into which the poet has been beaten by the conventional mores which he abhors. It also means pulse, the jazz rhythms which he believes are the true pulse of the time. Jack Kerouac says he invented the term and that it means "beatitude."

The beat poets are sometimes called the "New Bohemians" but, as the critic Norman Podhoretz has said, their bohemianism is very different from the 1920's variety. The older bohemianism "represented a repudiation of the provinciality, philistinism, and moral hypocrisy of American life." Its ideals were intelligence and cultivation. According to Mr. Podhoretz, the bohemianism of the fifties is "hostile to civilization; it worships primitivism, instinct, energy, blood."

The main difficulty in talking about the beat poets is to know where to find them. They have a way of vanishing upward into respectability or outward into silence. The most notorious of the group is Allen Ginsberg, whose "Howl" got itself banned for alleged obscenity in Chicago and San Francisco. Several of its verses suggest the justice of the charge, but its opening lines are chaste enough and are by now well known.

I saw the best minds of my generation destroyed by madness, starv-
ing hysterical naked,
dragging themselves through the negro streets at dawn looking for
an angry fix,
angelheaded hipsters burning for the ancient heavenly connection
to the starry dynamo in the machinery of night,
who poverty and tatters and hollow-eyed and high sat up smoking
in the supernatural darkness of cold-water flats floating across
the tops of cities contemplating jazz,
who bared their brains to Heaven under the El and saw Moham-
medan angels staggering on tenement roofs illuminated,
who passed through universities with radiant cool eyes hallucinating
Arkansas and Blake-light tragedy among the scholars of war,
who were expelled from the academies for crazy & publishing obscene odes on the windows of the skull,
who cowered in unshaven rooms in underwear, burning their money
in wastebaskets and listening to the Terror through the wall,
who got busted in their pubic beards returning through Laredo with
a belt of marijuana for New York,
who ate fire in paint hotels or drank turpentine in Paradise Alley,
death, or purgatoried their torsos night after night

And so on, through four sections, stretched over thirteen pages
of orgiastic verse, celebrating, as one critic has said, "the intellectual outlaw—that highbrow cousin of the black jacket,
switch-blade-toting street-fighter." While the critics have been
abusing "Howl" in this fashion, it has been selling. There were
eight printings between October 1956 and September 1959.

"Howl" is published in the Pocket Poets Series of the City
Lights Bookshop in San Francisco, one of the centers of the
New Bohemianism. City Lights also issues poetry by Gregory
Corso and Lawrence Ferlinghetti, the proprietor of City
Lights. Corso has not written much verse. I know of only three
volumes and they are slender: *The Vestal Lady on Brattle*
(that is, Brattle Street in Cambridge, Massachusetts), *Gasoline*,
and *The Happy Birthday of Death*. Corso does not shout into
the wind as Ginsberg does. His verse comes nearer the beat's
ideal form of expression by imitating the spontaneous, ex-
plosive effects of jazz. His eye is quick and so is his ear. But
the hipster vocabulary which he uses is very limited and he
will need some new words soon.

Lawrence Ferlinghetti tells us on the cover of *A Coney Island of the Mind* that he has been working "toward a kind of street poetry . . . to get poetry out of the inner aesthetic sanctum and out of the classroom into the street. The poet has contemplated his navel too long, while the world walks by." Here are two of Ferlinghetti's "oral messages," taken from his "Junkman's Obbligato."

> Let us arise and go now
> under the city
> where ashcans roll
> and reappear in putrid clothes
> as the uncrowned underground kings
> of subway men's rooms.
> Let us feed the pigeons
> at the City Hall
> urging them to do their duty
> in the Mayor's office.
> Hurry up please it's time.
> The end is coming.
> Flash Floods
> Disasters in the sun
> Dogs unleashed
> Sister in the street
> her brassiere backwards.

*   *   *

> Let's cut out let's go
> into the real interior of the country
> where hockshops reign
> mere unblind anarchy upon us.
> The end is here
> but golf goes on at Burning Tree.
> It's raining it's pouring
> The Ole Man is snoring.
> Another flood is coming
> though not the kind you think.
> There is still time to sink
> and think.
> I wish to descend in society.
> I wish to make like free.
> Sing low sweet chariot
> Let us not wait for the cadillacs . . .

These must be "oral" since they were written to be spoken to the accompaniment of a jazz band. But what the "messages" are escapes me.

If one looks into the careers of some of the other poets published by City Lights Books, one is in for a surprise. Kenneth Rexroth's name is in the list, but he is no fledgling beatnik. With William Carlos Williams he has been a champion, until very recently, of the beats, but he was born in 1905 and his first volume of verse appeared in 1940. Kenneth Patchen is another City Lights favorite but he is now forty-nine years old and the author of twenty-five books.

Two other younger poets in the City Lights list, Robert Duncan and Denise Levertov, evince the tendency of avant-garde poets in any age to climb to respectability. Duncan is reviewed respectfully in *Poetry* and his verse is published in it. Denise Levertov has been praised by Rexroth as the best of the avant-garde poets but there is little experimentation in her verse. She simply does well what the free-verse writers of forty-five years ago were doing. An Englishwoman who married an American G.I., she had a considerable reputation before she came to this country.

When you look steadily at the raw poetry movement, it evaporates like a jellyfish on the hot sands. I could summon a few more names—Charles Olson (another aging beatnik), Robert Creeley, Judson Crews, Gil Orlovitz, for instance— but the beat poets grow old or are old when they assume beatness, or become respectable. As a movement it will be remembered, I believe, as an episode which for a time filled a vacuum.

Meanwhile a new generation of poets has come along who are accomplishing many of the things the beats profess, without resorting to jazz rhythms or formless verse or obscenities or imitations of folk poetry, whatever that can mean in this age of mass communications. Like the beats they are not interested in organized social protest. Their verse is intense and intensely personal without being limited to a minority culture. They delight in rendering objects exactly. Some of them explore the lower depths in cities. Above all, they wish their "cooked" poetry to be readily received by their readers. They are not opposed to the mass media, although they do not write specifically for them. Their heroes are not Eliot or Pound or Auden. They have organized no movement. The three of this group I wish to speak of probably do not know one another —Philip Booth, W. D. Snodgrass, and Galway Kinnell. All three were college educated (as were many of the beats, for that matter) and all have taught in colleges. They are all under forty; the avant-garde of the unbeat poets.

Booth is a pastoral poet and a New England poet, a poet of the sea and of love. His verse strikes to the heart at once. There are no impediments. Here is a love poem which is also a sea poem. He calls it "Adam."

I take thee now to be no other
than you are. In the raw weather
of Northeast storms, in summer meadows
run with only the seabirds' shadows,

I risk my naked and imperfect praise.
From noon to sunlit moon, the days
make ceremony of my quick desire.
Wave by wave, the gray stone shore

diminishes to sand, the known coast
ebbs: and we stand watching, crest
on blue and whitecap crest, who search
still for a tidal lovers' beach.

Yet never do quivering lovers touch
the secret place they join to reach;
at flood between them, love divides,
as barred islands by spring tides.

So must we, Eve, content ourselves
how close we came. At equinox, our lives
are time enough to love again,
between the loon call and the rain.

And there is world enough. I claim
this coast by giving it a name;
I give you this calm morning
as the first, without storm warning

in the cirrus sky. Fish and seal,
crab and beach-pea, breed original
in my mind: heather, starfish forms,
are mine. I love you by the terms

I make to give you. I wake to call
the osprey, tern, the slow-winged gull,
say all the sea's grave names, and build
with words this beach that is the world.

Booth has thus far published one volume: *Letter from a Distant Land*, 1957.

W. D. Snodgrass, whose first volume, *Heart's Needle* (1959), has been widely acclaimed, wears his heart on his sleeve, unashamedly. Yet his superb artistic control mutes the lyric cry in his poems and makes the emotion bearable. The content of his poetry seems to have been found almost entirely in his own experience, as in this poem.

The Operation

From stainless steel basins of water
They brought warm cloths and they washed me,
From spun aluminum bowls, cold Zephiran sponges, fuming;
Gripped in the dead yellow glove, a bright straight razor
Inched on my stomach, down my groin,
Paring the brown hair off. They left me
White as a child, not frightened. I was not
Ashamed. They clothed me, then,
In the thin, loose, light, white garments,
The delicate sandals of poor Pierrot,
A schoolgirl first offering her sacrament.

I was drifting, inexorably, on toward sleep.
In skullcaps, masked, in blue-green gowns, attendants
Towed my cart, afloat in its white cloths,
The body with its tributary poisons borne
Down corridors of the diseased, thronging:
The scrofulous faces, contagious grim boys,
The huddled families, weeping, a staring woman
Arched to her gnarled stick,—a child was somewhere
Screaming, screaming—then, blind silence, the elevator rising
To the arena, humming, vast with lights; blank hero,
Shackled and spellbound, to enact my deed.

Into flowers, into women, I have awakened.
Too weak to think of strength, I have thought all day,
Or dozed among standing friends. I lie in night, now,
A small mound under linen like the drifted snow.
Only by nurses visited, in radiance, saying, Rest.
Opposite, ranked office windows glare; headlamps, below,
Trace out our highways; their cargoes under dark tarpaulins,
Trucks climb, thundering, and sirens may
Wail for the fugitive. It is very still. In my brandy bowl
Of sweet peas at the window, the crystal world
Is inverted, slow and gay.

Galway Kinnell, in another first volume, *What a Kingdom It Was* (1960), ranges more widely for themes than Booth and Snodgrass. He commemorates his boyhood and youth, the many places he has lived, in this country and abroad, and the people he has known. He is a poet of the city as well as the country. None of the beat poets have brought us so close to the degraded poor who are crowded together in our urban multinationed ghettos. The long poem, "The Avenue Bearing the Initial of Christ into the New World," which furnishes in its last line the title to his volume, takes us through the days and nights in a little kingdom in New York City which has Avenue C for its eastern boundary, Seventh Street for its northern, and Houston Street for its southern. With a coolness which is always compassionate, Mr. Kinnell presents the fish market, the pushcarts laden with vegetables, the store signs in many languages, children at play, the burning of Gold's junkstore, the old crone who sells papers she cannot read, the ancient Negro who sits outside the Happy Days Bar and Grill and every once in a while breaks into a chant:

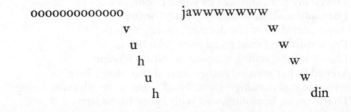

The fourteenth and last section of this notable poem sums up:

That night a wildcat cab whined crosstown on 7th.
You knew even the traffic lights were made by God,
The red splashes growing dimmer the farther away
You looked, and away up at 14th, a few green stars;
And without sequence, and nearly all at once,
The red lights blinked into green,
And just before there was one complete Avenue of green,
The little green stars in the distance blinked.

It is night and raining. You look down
Towards Houston in the rain, the living streets,
Where instants of transcendence
Drift in oceans of loathing and fear, like lanternfishes,
Or phosphorus flashings in the sea, or the feverish light
Skin is said to give off when the swimmer drowns at night.

From the blind gut Pitt to the East River of Fishes
The Avenue cobbles a swath through the discolored air,
A roadway of refuse from the teeming shores and ghettos
And the Caribbean Paradise, into the new ghetto and new paradise,
This God-forsaken Avenue bearing the initial of Christ
Through the haste and carelessness of the ages,
The sea standing in heaps, which keeps on collapsing,
Where the drowned suffer a C-change,
And remain the common poor.

Since Providence, for the realization of some unknown purpose, has
seen fit to leave this dangerous people on the face of the earth, and
did not destroy it . . .

Listen! the swish of the blood,
The sirens down the bloodpaths of the night,
Bone tapping on the bone, nerve-nets
Singing under the breath of sleep—
We scattered over the lonely seaways,
Over the lonely deserts did we run,
In dark lanes and alleys we did hide ourselves . . .

The lungs put out the light of the world as they
The heart beats without windows in its night,
Heave and collapse, the brain turns and rattles
In its own black axlegrease—

In the nighttime
Of the blood they are laughing and saying,
Our little lane, what a kingdom it was!

oi weih, oi weih

What one likes most about these three young poets (there are more of their breed) is the strong, directly expressed emotion in their verses. This may not yet be poetry for the people but it can be if the people will pause to listen.

Index